WHAT OBAMA MEANS

ALSO BY JABARI ASIM

The N Word: Who Can Say It,
Who Shouldn't, and Why

As Editor

Not Guilty: Twelve Black Men Speak Out on Law,
Justice, and Life

WHAT OBAMA MEANS

...FOR OUR CULTURE, OUR POLITICS, OUR FUTURE

JABARI ASIM

wm
WILLIAM MORROW
An Imprint of HarperCollins*Publishers*

HarperCollins books may be purchased for educational, business, or sales promotional use. For information please write: Special Markets Department, HarperCollins Publishers, 10 East 53rd Street, New York, NY 10022.

FIRST EDITION

Library of Congress Cataloging-in-Publication Data has been applied for.

ISBN 978-0-06-171133-6

09 10 11 12 13   OV/RRD   10 9 8 7 6 5 4 3 2 1

For Liana,
my smarter half

There are no accidents in my philosophy. Every effect must have its cause. The past is the cause of the present, and the present will be the cause of the future. All these are links in the endless chain stretching from the finite to the infinite.

ABRAHAM LINCOLN

Contents

WHAT
OBAMA
MEANS

PROLOGUE Convergence

WHEN I VISITED my mother last May, much of her living room had been converted into what I half jokingly called a Barack Obama shrine. Since Obama had declared his candidacy for president, my mother had diligently collected everything about the man that she could get her hands on. Magazines, newspaper articles, and T-shirts formed the bulk of her collection, all of it in pristine condition and not to be handled except with utmost care. Almost overnight, all things Obama had become a staple of my mother's conversation. His message of unity and transcendence, his unwillingness to be cowed by "a chorus of cynics," all of this inspired in my mother a late-life surge of confidence. It had even led to her changing the way she answered her phone. Instead of her usual "Hello," she took to lifting the receiver and announcing, "This is our moment."

By the night of Obama's remarkable triumph, she had digested far more than his trademark phrases. Still, she was more than thrilled when, during his victory speech at Chicago's Grant Park, he once again proclaimed, "This is our moment." Obama's victory seemed "just too good to be true, overwhelmingly good," she told me. "There are no words to describe how I feel. 'Elated' is not good enough."

Hers is a voice tempered and made scratchy by seventy-seven years of living, almost as many years of smoking, and decades of making herself heard in a house crowded with loud, boisterous youngsters. My mother is special to me, of course, but in many respects she's a typical black woman of her generation. A child of the Depression, she married young, stayed married, and stayed home to raise six children. She remembers Jim Crow quite well and, like many of her peers, has more than a few chilling firsthand tales of travel in Mississippi (where her father was born), Missouri, and other places known for white residents' historically open and often violent hostility toward African Americans. She is faithful, fearless, and frank, adept at blessing you with gentle encouragement while demonstrating her unerring skill at telling it exactly like it is. While her experience, her lifetime of dearly purchased knowledge, deeply informs my own life, there are parts of it to which I have no access. Her memories contain mysteries that I can only guess at. To hear her answer her phone with such an uncautiously optimistic phrase was a startling, wonderful surprise.

Her optimism, while inspired by Obama's meteoric rise, seems to me quite different from the youthful exuberance that often surrounded him. My mother remembers Emmett Till, Medgar, Malcolm, Martin—she's witnessed and endured enough to know that getting all giddy is foolish for colored people, let alone dangerous. But because she is a dedicated and informed voter, her hopefulness cannot be attributed to ignorance or naïveté. Nor does she choose to forget any of those traumas and tragedies. She can remember them while hoping at the same time.

To my knowledge, my mother has never mounted a soapbox and given a speech, never rocked the microphone at a street rally. She's one of those proud black Americans who could be relied on to fill seats when leaders like Martin Luther King Jr. came to town seeking support, applauding attentively and standing ready with the checkbook when a call for offerings was raised. I was with my mother when I saw Angela Davis speak at a rally during the distant seventies. I was sitting next to my mother when an aging Roy Wilkins presided over his last NAACP convention near the end of that decade. She supported them all, primarily because they were "race people," or dedicated champions of black advancement. And she clearly considers Barack

Obama a race man, the latest and most inspiring member of that exalted tradition.

———————

Others are less clear about Obama's place in the pantheon of exemplary black leadership or even whether he belongs at all. He complicates, in fascinating ways, conventional considerations of black political struggle.

At a forum I attended at Georgetown University last April, writers and thinkers gathered to discuss the legacy of the Black Arts Movement that deeply influenced African American creative culture in the 1960s. Although Obama was a child during that time, growing up far away from the poems, paintings, and music exploding in places like Newark, Harlem, and Watts, even that period had become difficult to discuss without working his campaign into the conversation.

Among the panelists were Amiri Baraka and Haki Madhubuti, celebrated poet-activists, race men, and former young lions turned gray eminences. "The mainstream is not ready for a fire-breathing black man," a friend of Obama's reportedly told the *New Yorker*. In contrast, fire-breathers have long been welcome in African American communities (see Wright, Rev. Jeremiah). In fact, anyone who aspired to leadership in the traditional sense was expected to at least suggest the potential for bringing the heat. Baraka and Madhubuti, to borrow the poet Jayne Cortez's term, are fire*spitters*. Baraka, a two-fisted bantamweight known for wailing his poems with the volume and magnetic intensity of a hard-bop saxophonist, had visibly mellowed, although he could still skillfully move a crowd and leaven his intensity with savage, witty ad-libs. While delivering his trademark denunciation of monopoly capitalism, he openly grappled with the "postrace" riddle, trying to determine Obama's relationship to a phrase the candidate had never officially embraced.

Madhubuti gave a variation of the speech I'd often heard him deliver when I was an awestruck college student, haunting his bookstore on Chicago's South Side and sitting attentively through lecture after lecture at Olive-Harvey community college's annual black studies conference. I still remember a chalk talk in which he demonstrated persuasively that the ministerial model of black leadership was insufficiently equipped to deal with an increasingly educated and sophisticated ruling class. Obama, educated and sophisticated, with a background in grassroots organizing, would seem to fit into the model of alternative leadership that Madhubuti was then proposing.

In the wake of the furor surrounding Obama's comments about "bitter" Americans, Madhubuti defended bitterness in American society and in black American communities in particular. Given the harsh conditions confronting so many of our people, he seemed to suggest, bitterness was understandable. His words reminded me of Malcolm X's witty response to those who called him an extremist. "I'm an extremist," he said, because the black race is in "extremely bad condition." Like Malcolm, Madhubuti takes care to address the concerns of the disenfranchised, the black people (usually in the inner cities) for whom all this talk of progress must often seem like a cruel joke.

Two weeks before the Georgetown event, economist Glenn C. Loury had made similar observations in an online column. Historically, the shape-shifting Loury has been as far away from Madhubuti on the ideological spectrum as Angela Davis is from Condoleezza Rice. But Madhubuti's comments at Georgetown echoed Loury's. Pointing out the wishful thinking behind the idea of a postrace society, Loury had noted, "As I write this, one million young black men are under the physical control of the state; a third of black children live in poverty, and, the Southside of Chicago, with more than one-half million black residents, is one of the most massive, racially segregated urban enclaves ever to have been created in the modern world."

Madhubuti, putting the lie to critics of race men who say they avoid talk of personal responsibility, went on to challenge black America's penchant for mindless consumption and apparent aversion to production and manufacturing. He was visibly angry as he spoke; part of his frustration seemed to come from his awareness that the substance of his speech had changed little over the years—not because he had no new ideas but because the conditions he addressed had remained largely the same. Some problems had shown little to no improvement in the past forty years (17 percent unemployment, 50 percent dropout rate), while others had gotten distressingly worse (79 percent of black babies born outside of marriage, skyrocketing incarceration rates for black males).

Abolitionist William Lloyd Garrison once complained that his initial efforts to "excite the minds of the people" about the antislavery cause had been "palsied by public indifference." A similar plague of apathy seems to complicate the efforts of veteran activists like Madhubuti; indeed the reluctance of the disadvantaged to get "excited" over the prospect of reaching escape velocity seems to be just as formidable as the systemic racism that hinders their rise. Madhubuti knows this and it doesn't make him happy.

In his essay, Loury expressed aloud the conundrum at the heart of the race man's dilemma—an irritating question that Americans in general are frequently hesitant to address: What is our proper relationship with history?

Madhubuti and Baraka struck me that day as living history. Once allies who angrily split over fierce ideological differences, the two men had grown comfortable enough with each other in recent years to share podiums and work on books together. Their durable bond and stalwart presence in black intellectual circles suggested that having in common a ferocious passion for black advancement was sufficient reason to join forces—in much the same way, perhaps, as Obama's invocation of hope insists that that emotion alone can help us overcome our stubborn differences.

Sitting in the audience at Georgetown, I identified with the speakers as they parsed recent events for clues to reading our changing cultural geography in the age of Obama. Though my dalliance with black nationalism was brief and I was never even tempted by Marxism—two poles that Madhubuti and Baraka once represented—I clung to the perhaps romantic notion of myself as a race man in the old-fashioned sense of the term. Indeed, in black thought the idea of the race man transcended "isms" and included a vast range of wildly varying and occasionally disparate political philosophies, including W. E. B. DuBois's Pan-Africanism, Paul Robeson's unabashed internationalism, and the earnest integrationism of Walter White and Roy Wilkins. Malcolm X, Langston Hughes—race men both. Even Ralph Ellison, stern and unapproachable in his Riverside Drive apartment, with ever-loyal Fannie guarding the door, was a race man in his way. If we cast its gender-specificity aside, the concept—if not the phrase—has been expansive enough to embrace brilliant leaders of the feminine persuasion, such as Fannie Lou Hamer, Ella Baker, Ida B. Wells.

Booker T. Washington, too. "It is sad to think of a man without a country," he once observed. "It is sadder to think of a man without a race."

Where Washington implied a belief in race loyalty and

obligation, his fierce rival DuBois declared his mission outright. He spelled it out in a 1902 essay, "Of the Training of Black Men": "I insist that the question of the future is how best to keep these millions [9 million Negroes] from brooding over the wrongs of the past and the difficulties of the present, so that all their energies may be bent toward a cheerful striving and cooperation with their white neighbors toward a larger, juster, and fuller future."

How does a race man regard his mission amid the shifting winds of the millennial age? Is he confused? Sullen? Precisely how large, just, and full is the future looking these days, and how has Obama changed its scope—if at all? Obama's bold election night declaration seemed aimed squarely at such questions. "It's been a long time coming," he asserted, "but tonight, because of what we did on this day, in this election, at this defining moment, change has come to America."

According to Edward Said, intellectual performances can "keep in play both the sense of opposition and the sense of engaged participation." That's what modern race men and women do at their best. At once fiercely critical and resolutely patriotic, they've got too much blood in this soil, ancestral ties too tenacious to ever consider packing their bags. "I love America more than any other country in the world, and, exactly for this reason, I insist on the right to criticize her perpetually," James Baldwin wrote. With the heyday of Parisian exile long gone and journeys back to

Africa exposed as mostly implausible, race men and women have nowhere else to go. There are too many bodies in the earth, and you can't, as Toni Morrison once wrote, just up and leave a body. Those bones belong to the land, the land belongs to us, and we don't need to wear lapel pins to prove it.

In a *Newsweek* article about Obama, Evan Thomas uncharitably and inaccurately dismissed "race men" (the quotes are his) as old-style politicians "who use skin color as a political tool." That's a superficial and woefully ahistorical view that fails to take into account African America's rich tradition of strategic resistance and constructive dissent. The skepticism with which race men can be counted on to challenge our historically sluggish government is ultimately a quintessential *American* impulse. After all, they merely put into practice the necessary vigilance that Tom Paine described long ago. "Common sense will tell us," he argued, "that the power which hath endeavoured to subdue us, is of all others, the most improper to defend us."

Malcolm X, among the most eloquent of the dissenters, insisted that black Americans had to get their own houses in order before engaging their white countrymen at the bargaining table. He returned again and again to the need "to instill within black men the racial dignity, the incentive, and the confidence that the black race needs today to get up off its knees, and to get on its feet, and get rid of its scars, and to take a stand for itself."

Race leaders not only advocate on behalf of blacks but "at the same time needle, cajole, and denounce Negroes themselves for inertia, diffidence, and lack of race pride," St. Clair Drake and Horace Cayton noted in their 1945 landmark book, *Black Metropolis*. So deeply ingrained is this self-correcting strand (the politics of black respectability) that both black and white comedians have subjected it to blistering parody. For example, on NBC's *30 Rock* Tracy Morgan costars as Tracy Jordan, a talented actor given to fits of paranoia. He tries to stay one step ahead of a "secret group of powerful black Americans" he calls the Black Crusaders. According to his delusion, members of the cabal (including Bill Cosby, Oprah Winfrey, Colin Powell, and Gordon from *Sesame Street*) meet "four times a year in the skull of the Statue of Liberty," where they make plans to "ruin anybody who they think are making black people look bad."

Critics of African American liberalism sometimes miss the whole responsibility thing, or pretend that it simply doesn't exist as an element of the black progressive agenda. Shelby Steele, to provide one ironic example, appears not to recognize how closely his own words sometimes resemble Malcolm's. "You must never ever concede that only black responsibility can truly lift blacks into parity with whites. . . . If blacks should be responsible for their own uplift, then it is not racist for whites to expect them to do so," Steele offered in *A Bound Man*. He writes as if DuBois, Marcus

Garvey ("Up you mighty race!"), and Malcolm had never spoken—frequently and eloquently—on such matters. Left unanswered in Steele's critique is why the measured rise of black professionals, as admirable a demonstration of responsibility as any, has thus far failed to result in any semblance of parity extending beyond the middle class.

To his credit, however, Steele correctly anticipated the grumbling that arose in some quarters of black thought when Obama occasionally gave speeches criticizing absentee black fathers, negligent mothers, and other forms of malignant conduct among African Americans. Some critics wondered why Obama singled out blacks when those misbehaviors occur among other ethnic groups as well. For a race man to ask such a question is especially odd, since Obama was merely paying attention to an unavoidable fact that race men are obligated to point out: where black Americans are concerned, there is always more at stake. Some folks seemed to understand this more readily than Jesse Jackson did, for Obama's comments last Father's Day at Chicago's Apostolic Church lowered his standing among black voters not one bit.

Malcolm X seldom drew such criticism when he made similar comments.

Malcolm's context and constituency may have differed dramatically from those of a black man with his eye on the presidency, but Obama clearly understands that little else has changed in terms of the internal difficulties that blacks face and the role of self-sabotage in making them worse. Nor has Obama missed the connection between the improbable journeys of men like Malcolm and his own unlikely emergence. He has written that Malcolm's "repeated acts of self-creation" spoke to him as a young man. Malcolm had to become a citizen of the world before he could see that the battle for civil rights was a battle for human rights. Obama, by birthright and upbringing, grew up a citizen of the world and thus was able to conclude much earlier, "the hopes of the little girl who goes to a crumbling school in Dillon are the same as the dreams of the boy who learns on the streets of L.A."

It's the very fragility of those dreams that prompts such caution among African Americans who've left younger days behind. The memory of dreams deferred leads to a wary perspective that tempts outsiders to dismiss it as unqualified cynicism, but watchfulness may be a better word. After Emancipation, when unshackled jubilation gave way to anguish following the crushing end of Reconstruction, black Americans were forced to reconsider the wages of optimism. "The slave went free," DuBois wrote, "stood a brief moment in the sun; then moved back again toward slavery." Hence a collective guardedness that sometimes has no basis other than an awareness that freedom can be snatched away if it is not fiercely defended.

Do I believe the relative prosperity of the black middle class (relative to their poor black counterparts; the wealth gap between black and white middle-class Americans remains alarmingly large), Obama's historic victory, and other notable advances will amount to just another brief moment in the sun? No, I don't, but our history here forcefully reminds us that we will always—*always*—need some individuals among us willing to watch our backs.

That's where race men and women come in—not the charlatans and camera hogs with whom we are all too familiar, but those genuinely dedicated to service and uplift. As long as racial disparities exist, as long as there are problems particular to black people, loyal advocacy is not only desired but also required.

Obama has said as much himself. He writes in *The Audacity of Hope* that for black Americans, "separation from the poor is never an option, and not just because the color of our skin—and the conclusions the larger society draws from our color—makes all of us only as free, only as respected, as the least of us."

Whether racism is the root cause of our problems is almost beside the point: such issues demand the concentrated attention of men and women who will go at them with ferocity, intelligence, and love.

But try mentioning the value of vigilance to young black people—whether poor or prosperous—and their eyes may glaze over before you finish your first sentence. Try telling the bright, accomplished, and privileged black undergrads at Georgetown that black people are "in trouble," as Madhubuti did, and you get mostly polite silence. One can't help contrasting that response with the mobs of bright, accomplished, and privileged young black people who have taken to Obama and his message with such enthusiasm.

Obama, as might be expected, has paid tribute to youth spirit at every opportunity. When the forces of doubt threaten to slow him down, he says, what gives him hope is "the next generation—the young people whose attitudes and beliefs and openness to change have already made history in this election."

He has made no mention of the racial makeup of this youth brigade, for many of whom "race" has taken on the most fluid connotations ever found in the United States. The very notion of a "post-sixties black identity," to borrow Shelby Steele's convenient phrase, may be an all but alien concept to an African American born in, say, 1987. Members of the Millennial Generation, usually defined as born between 1982 and 2003, are "the most ethnically diverse generation in American history," "more positive than older generations both about the present and future state of their own lives and about the future of their country," and "united across gender and race in their desire to find 'win-win' solutions to America's problems," according to Morley Winograd and Michael D. Hais, authors of *Millennial Makeover: MySpace, YouTube, and the Future of American Politics.*

And, having grown up during an era in which unparalleled technological breakthroughs have enabled a remarkable outpouring of creativity, they are far more likely to take their cues from video-sharing or social networking sites than from America's past. Years ago, I scoffed when rapper Chuck D called rap music black America's CNN. I still don't think his analogy was on the money, but watching today's young people effortlessly manipulate their smartphones, iPods, and digital doodads, at last I'm beginning to get what he meant about alternative modes of communication. Of course, in the twenty-first century the alternative has become the standard. It's not a hip-hop world anymore (if it ever was), and these passionate, politically engaged youth are not members of the hip-hop generation. Russell Simmons is in his fifties now (older than Obama), and the rapper on the mic is almost as likely to be an Indian American, Samoan, or Latino as an African American from Boogie Down Bronx or Compton, California. They make beats, spit rhymes, create images, and spout lingo amid an intoxicating, ever-expanding, mind-boggling datastream that knows no boundaries, geographic or cultural. Thirty years after Parliament-Funkadelic raised the possibility, Millennials need only push a button or tap a keyboard to go "all around the world for the funk."

While race men have been cultural watchdogs—Jesse Jackson has periodically weighed in against the misogyny and profane language expressed in hip-hop music—while simultaneously practicing some of those activities himself, namely, adultery and calling black people "niggas"—they have largely missed many of the potentially transformative developments in popular culture. Amiri Baraka, for example, lectured his Georgetown audience on the need for a national black newspaper, as if Web 2.0 had never happened and black journalists had not responded with online news sites such as TheDailyVoice.com, TheRoot.com, and EbonyJet.com.

This new version of youth spirit doesn't just confound African Americans who grew up in a society largely defined by race. Members of the majority culture have often failed to recognize and respond to the generation's cues. For example, when Hillary Clinton adviser Mark Penn suggested that Obama's supporters "looked like Facebook," he indicated his own failure to grasp the rapid changes taking place. Like many of us, he just didn't get it.

Obama apparently did. He stated, "One of my fundamental beliefs from my days as a community organizer is that real change comes from the bottom up. And there's no more powerful tool for grass-roots organizing than the Internet." His prescience led to My.BarackObama.com, a website shaped by Chris Hughes, a cofounder of Facebook. It helped him turn the world of political organizing on its head, raising more than 2 million donations of less than two hundred dollars each. Hughes was all of twenty-four at the time.

The self-generating, DIY philosophy behind such ventures is hardly new. But powered by Internet technology, it can popularize and spread an idea (for instance, that Obama should be president) like brushfire. With no input from the candidate, in February 2008 Will.i.am, music producer and front man of the Black Eyed Peas, created a "Yes We Can" video, a moving blend of music and testimony (mostly from young, good-looking celebrities) that turned out to be far more effective than a paid advertising spot.

According to the Associated Press, Will.i.am's video "quickly went viral" and "drew its one millionth hit within a few days of being posted." By June, according to the *New York Times,* the video had been "viewed more than 18 million times, first at YouTube, and now at the Obama campaign's portal, my.barackobama.com." Although he and his band had performed at John Kerry fund-raisers during the 2004 race, Will.i.am considered himself mostly apolitical. Then he heard Obama's address following the New Hampshire primary and everything changed. The speech, he wrote, "inspired me to want to change myself to better the world . . . and take a 'leap' towards change . . . and hope that others become inspired to do the same."

Will.i.am's response to Obama's words—and its immediate impact upon popular culture—illustrates what sociologist Robert Putnam calls "areas of convergence." Putnam suggests that there are more of these areas than Americans realize, and that Obama was perfectly suited to capitalize upon them for the nation's benefit. "We feel divided in racial terms, religious terms, class terms, all kinds of terms, but we exaggerate how much we disagree with each other,"

Putnam told the *New Yorker.* "And that's why I think he's right for this time."

Convergence—a ground-level version of the harmonic kind—is also the word that kept coming to my mind when I began to observe Obama's phenomenal rise. I attributed it to the alignment of irreversible cultural trends, substantial political developments, and unstoppable market forces. None of that is meant to diminish the man himself: his charisma, his peerless eloquence, his seemingly effortless mastery of the issues, and the clarity with which he presents and pursues his agenda. But none of those qualities counters the fact that he appeared at exactly the right time and place in the course of American events. Although Obama's very ascendance is a watershed moment, it has set in motion consequences that will reach far beyond his presidency. In addition to turning the old civil rights model of African American leadership on its head in ways that I don't think even Obama foresaw, he has suggested a new framework of public service and leadership that will undoubtedly influence ambitious Americans of all backgrounds.

It's likely that none of that was on Will.i.am's mind in February 2008, when he followed his first Obama project with another music video, "We Are The Ones." Its large, telegenic cast included nineteen-year-old Zoë Kravitz, a singer-actress and daughter of musician Lenny Kravitz, whose whole career seems rooted in the kind of global-harmony vibes aroused by Obama's emergence.

Zoë Kravitz's onscreen comments following the video

sum up the rising tide of sentiment—exuberantly free of old neuroses—that helped Obama's campaign go from a long-shot venture to one of our nation's most memorable and stirring quests for higher office. And they provide some hint of a new social compact flexible enough to inspire my seventy-seven-year-old mother in the Midwest and a nineteen-year-old in Hollywood.

"I want to be an optimistic person," Zoë said, "and Barack is helping me do that."

CHAPTER 1
What Cool Can Do

A **YOUNG MAN** grows up as the only son of a white mother and a brilliant, misunderstood black father who has drowned his early promise in drink. The young man broods a lot and hones his craft amid a multicultural crowd of energetic young people. Despite being clearly talented, he attracts critics who suggest that he's overly ambitious, just a kid. Perhaps he should set his sights a little lower, bide his time. He struggles, endures unfulfilling relationships, experiments with self-destructive behavior. In the end, though, he prevails. He mounts the stage amid great expectations and leaves it to great applause.

If you've seen *Purple Rain,* Prince's 1984 Oscar-winning film, the plot I've described is quite familiar to you.

Any resemblance between Barack Obama's real-life story and Prince's fictional one is entirely coincidental. After all, Prince starred in that big-screen musical long before most of us had ever heard of Obama. But its biracial themes and Prince's aggressive pursuit of a multiracial image bear closer observance. For in many ways, the path to success pursued by Prince, Michael Jackson, and black performers who have followed their trail anticipated—and helped pave—the road that Obama traveled on his way to the White House. What's more, the world they describe—one free of racial obsessions—closely resembles the American society that Obama calls for and that his followers enthusiastically applaud.

There were successful multiracial bands before Prince and the Revolution hit the scene, and their two-tone racial makeup has been as much a subject of historical discussion as the quality of the music they produced. Still, in a society constricted by Jim Crow laws and customs that governed concert halls, hotels, railroads, radio stations, and more, there's no question that those early bands desegregated at considerable risk. Benny Goodman took a big chance when he added Lionel Hampton and Teddy Wilson to his band in the mid-1930s, a time when racial separation was intensely observed in popular music.

Decades later, when Jimi Hendrix emerged as a guitarist of singular gifts, the risks were still there. Having honed his skills on the "chitlin' circuit" as a sideman with various black R & B outfits, Hendrix gained fame as an international rock star after woodshedding in England. He electrified a genre and redefined expectations in much the same manner as guitarist Charlie Christian did when he joined forces with the Goodman band. But unlike Christian, Hendrix was front and center, the obvious leader of a trio that, initially, was otherwise all white. While white fans mostly embraced him, some grumbling arose in black communities. A thread of criticism arose that Obama would find nauseatingly familiar: Hendrix, some said, wasn't "black enough."

By 1969, Hendrix "was said to be under pressure from black militants seeking to interest him in political causes," according to *The Rolling Stone Illustrated History of Rock & Roll*. He found himself in another predicament to which Obama has been no stranger. Stuck between constituencies, "he was clearly caught in yet another situation where he wanted to please everybody, and was willing to stretch himself to do so."

Sly and the Family Stone, contemporaries of Hendrix whose influence continues into the present, encountered less resistance to their integrated lineup. Outrageous where Hendrix was soft-spoken, the charismatic Stone often overwhelmed his critics. In songs like "Everyday People" and "You Can Make It If You Try," he charmed black and white audiences alike with his relentless, upbeat funk. "You Can Make It If You Try," repeated like a mantra against a driving backdrop of brass, drums, bass, and electric keys, is both a highly danceable exhortation and a timely kick in the pants, roughly equal to saying "Yes We Can" while also acknowledging the need for personal effort and responsibility. Like Will.i.am's creation, it's an ode to optimism, the seeds of which, after a long gestation, are finally beginning to blossom. As hard as it may be to imagine, admirers described Stone in language reminiscent of that found in various profiles of Obama.

"Sly was a philosopher, preaching a message of total reconciliation," notes veteran rock writer Dave Marsh. In his persuasive view, Stone's approach "could heal all wounds," providing whites and blacks with "a meeting ground where they could work out their mistrust."

In so doing, musicians like Stone, for all their flamboyance and flouting of convention, ultimately performed a patriotic service. (Hendrix, a veteran of the 101st Airborne, talked with Dick Cavett about his astonishing, revisionist "Star-Spangled Banner" on Cavett's late-night talk show. "All I did was play it," he explained. "I'm an American, so I played it.") Through their lyrics and integrated lineups, and in casting a spotlight on audience members of various hues dancing and clapping to the same beat, they supplied critical cues to generations growing up under their influence. Undoubtedly their audiences included Americans wrestling with questions of identity and belonging that define both our individual and national quests. Or, as Obama put it when discussing his own life, "I learned to slip back and forth between my black and white worlds, understanding that each possessed its own language and customs and structures of meaning, convinced that with a bit of translation on my part the two worlds would eventually cohere."

By creating a common melody from those fragments of culture, Stone, Hendrix, and other like-minded musicians revealed tantalizing glimpses of a more perfect union.

Building on their efforts, Prince took calculated aim at "crossover" success. As Obama has done in politics, he avoided identifying explicitly with race by forgoing an explicitly "black" sound, deemphasizing bass and horns, and eventually favoring a rock-flavored electric guitar over his earlier, synth-based recordings. After he straightened the bushy Afro he wore for his first album cover, Prince successfully crossed over from the R & B charts, scoring a pair of top ten pop hits. A few albums later he started wearing neo-Edwardian costumes, was named *Rolling Stone*'s Artist of the Year, and copped an Academy Award. On the way to that trip to the podium, Prince successfully advanced the idea of a raceless utopia enriched by confidence, sensuality, and rhythm—or, as he put it in "Uptown," "Black, White, Puerto Rican, everybody just a-freakin'." His concerts amassed dancing fans of all ethnic varieties in an orgy of powerful, occasionally conflicting impulses—sex, salvation, and rebellion—that he somehow made work. All the while he toyed with a shape-shifting racial—and sexual—identity. "Am I black or white?" he asked in "Controversy." "Am I straight or gay?"

At fifty, Prince is just a few years older than Obama. His upbringing in Minnesota doesn't at first sound comparable to Obama's in Hawaii, but it seems likely that they sifted among the same pop-cultural products as they suffered the challenges of adolescence. For Obama, TV, movies, and radio supplied "an arcade of images from which you could cop a walk, a talk, a step, a style." Along with books, he also consulted these sources for information about the sixties—information that differed from the facts and stories his mother had shared. In *The Audacity of Hope,* he discusses how such exposure to pop culture helped him cop not only a walk and a talk but an attitude as well.

"If I had no immediate reasons to pursue revolution, I decided nevertheless that in style and attitude I, too, could be a rebel, unconstrained by the received wisdom of the over-thirty crowd," he writes. He sounds as if he could have easily fit in with the youthful multitudes bustin' a move at First Avenue, the Minneapolis club where much of *Purple Rain* takes place. When young rebels arrive at middle age, they sometimes find themselves in unlikely places. Knocking on the door of the White House, for example, or knocking on doors, as Prince does, as a member of the Jehovah's Witnesses.

For all his lyrics about sex and God, Prince has also been a steady critic of the military-industrial complex. He worried, for instance, about nuclear proliferation in "1999" ("Mommy, why does everybody have a bomb?") and lambasted the Strategic Defense Initiative in his hit "Sign o' the Times" ("Baby make a speech, Star Wars fly"). Although Prince's faith is believed to have prevented him from commenting on the election, he managed to sneak in a timely dig now and then. And they're consistent with both his and Obama's antiwar message.

"I'm so tired of debates, I don't know what to do," he announced to the crowd at the Coachella Valley Music and Arts Festival last April. "We're going to beat the swords into plowshares tonight."

It may be comments like those that prompted the formation of an online group called Prince Fans for Obama. When I visited the group's website last September, it had sixty-six members. It is "dedicated to the belief that if Prince wasn't apathetic towards voting due to his religion, he would vote for Barack Obama. Furthermore, we believe that Barack Obama upholds the ideals set forth by Prince in every way." Talk about improbable journeys.

A former Jehovah's Witness himself, Michael Jackson spent much of the eighties establishing a pop-culture kingdom and has spent much of every decade since tearing it down. Between 1980, when he won a Grammy for his recording of "Don't Stop 'Til You Get Enough," and 1993, when a lawsuit accused him of sexually molesting a thirteen-year-old boy, Jackson's landmark *Thriller* album earned platinum status twenty-one times, making it the best-selling LP in history. Although Jackson's public conduct became increasingly off the wall, his work throughout reflected an awareness of social inequality and injustice. More so than Prince's, Jackson's work suggests an ongoing engagement with real-life concerns and a defiant optimism that problems can and will be overcome. Whereas Obama's twenty-first-century evocation of hope has encouraged Americans to get out and vote, Jackson's rhythm-driven tracks urged them to get up and dance. Still, the parallels are readily apparent. In "Can You Feel It," a valediction forbidding hate, Jackson argues, "The blood inside of me is inside of you." In *The Audacity of Hope,* Obama encourages us to honor "a tradition based on the simple idea that we have a stake in each other." Jackson sings, "We are the world"; Obama declares, "we are the ones we have been waiting for." In "Heal the World," Jackson urges us to "make it a better place"; Obama's speech declaring his candidacy talks about "building a better America." In "Man in the Mirror," Jackson's most stirring call to action, the fiery chorus urges listeners to "make that . . . change!" Accepting his party's nomination in Denver last August, Obama announced, "It's time for us to change America."

Of course, other singers and bands have expressed similar themes, but because none has come close to selling 40 million copies of their recordings, their influence cannot be compared to Jackson's. Just as few performers (if any) can lay claim to influencing notions of racial conciliation to the degree that Jackson has, no political figure since Martin Luther King Jr. has forged alliances across racial boundaries with the skill and impact that Obama has shown.

In a video version of "Man in the Mirror" based on a Jackson concert tour of Europe and Asia, footage of the singer onstage is interspersed with shots of white women so transfixed by their proximity to the singer that they scream, cry, and faint. As security personnel swoop in and lift the limp women above the heads of the ecstatic multitudes, Jackson commands the audience to look inside themselves and make a change. Meanwhile, flickering images of Gandhi, John F. Kennedy, Martin Luther King Jr., and other historical figures alternate between scenes of Jackson driving his audience to ever-increasing frenzy. The video, shot during a tour that reached more than 4 million fans across 123 dates, perfectly captures the apotheosis of the pop star as a global figure on a par with religious leaders and heads of state.

Although Jackson's message of healing and change is shown to be salve for the soul, the women listeners' behavior suggests it is also sustenance for the libido. As in Prince's message, the distance between salvation and sensual bliss is obliterated. The satirical Obama Girl video and campaign buttons declaring Hot Chicks Dig Obama suggest that

Obama's appearances have aroused similar, albeit unsought connections—an unavoidable possibility, perhaps, when one considers that Obama is, while not the youngest, certainly the sleekest and most stylish presidential candidate in some time, if not ever. Obama has been particularly defensive about attempts to portray him as sexually attractive. During the campaign he and his staff discouraged such chatter by referring to him as a "skinny kid with big ears and a funny name."

Before his long fall, Jackson was the most beloved pop figure in the world and therefore, like Obama, dramatically expanded the horizons of black possibility. As Jackson stood before vast audiences with arms outstretched, basking in the glow of their adoration, he seemed to have brought DuBois's hope for black musicians to its fullest realization.

For DuBois, singing wasn't just about hitting the right notes but about providing a model for the rest of the planet while undoing stereotypes of black inferiority. "It is to be trusted," he wrote, "that our leaders in music, holding on to the beautiful heritage of the past, will not on that account, either be coerced or frightened from taking all music for their province and showing the world how to sing."

Seldom have black musicians done otherwise. Slaves brought with them instruments and techniques from Africa that amazed and delighted the plantation owners whom they were forced to entertain. These included Thomas Jefferson, who, in addition to being a Founding Father, was an early and influential advocate of white supremacy. Naturally, Jefferson found little to praise in blacks but was somehow able to acknowledge, "In music they are more generally gifted than the whites with accurate ears for tune and time." However, he cautioned, "Whether they will be equal to the composition of a more extensive run of melody, or of complicated harmony, is yet to be proved."

The ability to prove such skills during slavery was difficult, to say the least. After Emancipation, the Fisk Jubilee Singers, formed in 1871 to help save a foundering school for Negroes in Nashville, Tennessee, put doubts such as Jefferson's to rest. Over the course of nearly seven years, they performed in northern cities and in Europe, including a private concert for President Ulysses S. Grant. They raised more than $150,000 (more than $2.5 million in today's dollars), helping build Fisk University into a world-class institution that would later open its doors to a young student named W. E. B. DuBois when Harvard would not. In addition, they were civil rights activists before such activism had a name. Defying attempts to confine them to segregated audiences and accommodations, they demanded and received treatment as first-class citizens. Just as important, with their demanding repertoire (joyfully free of minstrelsy) and exacting performances, they served as highly effective globe-trotting cultural ambassadors on behalf of black equality. "Their music made all other vocal music cheap," enthused a fan named Mark Twain. "In the Jubilees and their songs, America has produced the perfectest flower of the ages."

Just as Obama has made spectacular use of new Internet technology, musicians in the twentieth century took their works to the world in ways that the Fisk Jubilee Singers couldn't have dreamed of. As a result, African American music, and the ways to distribute it, helped the image of black artists not only become popular but also attain a degree of influence that far exceeded their number.

White allies played a critical role. A typical effort, a 1938 Carnegie Hall concert called "From Spirituals to Swing," presented, in the words of its promoter, "talented Negro artists from all over the country who had been denied entry to the white world of white music." Such venues, along with the sprouting of recording studios, radio stations, and record shops, as well as developments in portrait photography and design, helped musicians such as Lester Young, Duke Ellington, and Billie Holiday become iconic figures. The bebop pioneers that followed, especially Charlie "Bird" Parker and Dizzie Gillespie, helped usher in a new age in which "hipness" became an American attribute to be desired. Similarly, the lingo favored by jazzmen and others in black communities became a desirable sign of pop-culture awareness.

"Cool" jazz followed, coming on the heels of bebop in the late 1940s. Many of the composers and arrangers of the music were white musicians from the West Coast. Cool was a hybrid of styles including the smoothness of Lester Young and fast tempos from the beboppers who came after him. It was essentially a two-toned music, but black performers such as Miles Davis became the public face of it. Besides adding another aspect of cool to the ferociously hip persona perfected by the hard-blowing beboppers, jazz musicians influenced developments in literature, fashion, advertising, and other cultural categories.

For many of them, landing a recording deal with Blue Note Records was definite, delightful proof that one had arrived. The Blue Note album covers of the fifties and sixties are still treasured today as examples of elegant design. Featuring dapper artists such as Hank Mobley, Dexter Gordon, and Lee Morgan, they conveyed an image of black men as stylish, cerebral, and undeniably masculine. On Gordon's *Our Man In Paris,* showing him with a thinly knotted tie, a collar bar, a hint of houndstooth lapel, and a cigarette (this was 1963), the saxophonist exudes a man-of-the-world confidence similar to Obama's on the *Ebony* magazine cover discussed below.

These men had a look, an aura, that white men didn't hesitate to copy. Like the smoke rising from a jazzer's everpresent cigarette, the possibility that blackness wasn't so bad floated out of the dives and nightclubs and into the open air.

Few spread more fumes than the photogenic and subversively charismatic Miles Davis. Davis released *Birth of the Cool* in 1957, but it was recorded in 1949–1950, while

Jack Kerouac was wandering the streets of Denver. In *On the Road,* Kerouac recalls walking through a black section of that city in 1949, "wishing I were a Negro, feeling the best the white world had offered was not enough ecstasy for me, not enough life, joy, kicks, darkness, music, not enough night."

The vapors Kerouac inhaled had been in the air awhile, even if they hadn't spread very far from the epicenter of jazz. In the 1930s, Jeffrey Melnick writes in *A Right to Sing the Blues,* Jewish musicians had tried to "capture some of the masculine cachet stereotypically ascribed to the black male." In the 1920s, Mezz Mezzrow, a Jewish musician, declared himself a "voluntary Negro" dedicated to "hipping the world about the blues the way only Negroes can." Kerouac and the Beats were also a comparatively marginalized group (and included Jews), so their infatuation with black culture needn't be taken as a mainstream development. What's more, like the hipsters in Norman Mailer's 1957 essay "The White Negro," who "drifted out at night looking for action with a black man's code to fit their facts," their concepts of blackness often seem rooted more in their imaginations than in reality. Nonetheless, they helped make it possible for white Americans to not only openly admire what they perceived as black cool but also declare their aspirations to get some of it for themselves. If the concept of cool hadn't yet become one of the many facets permanently attached to black identity, it certainly was by the end of the 1950s.

Jazz had a brief, sweet heyday and was soon supplanted by R & B and rock and roll. African American standouts in these jukebox-friendly genres tended to be raucous and raunchy, far less concerned with dignity and sophistication than their jazz counterparts. Even so, they also challenged whites' reluctance to overcome their prejudices.

"Although they hardly get their due, black rock and roll artists helped establish the idea of black humanity in a large white fan base," Michael Eric Dyson has noted. "Without Chuck Berry's 1955 'Maybelline' and Little Richard's 'Tutti Frutti' the same year, all that came after them, including Elvis, makes no sense." The majority of white citizens might not have been willing to invite Negroes into their homes just yet, but they didn't hesitate to buy their records and attend their performances.

Next came the Motown era, during which head honcho Berry Gordy produced one chart-topper after another from his Hitsville recording studio in Detroit. With superstars like Marvin Gaye and the Temptations effortlessly mixing elegance and alert social commentary with relaxed, soulful harmonies, the label kept alive the notion of cool even while tempers ran hot and urban streets went up in flames. It seemed to make perfect sense when Gordy, intentionally shaping the sound of the swelling black inner cities into a more palatable—and wildly popular—form, began to market his label's music as "the sound of young America."

Michael Jackson came of age in Gordy's hit factory,

when songs were still introduced to the public via 45 rpm singles. He became a superstar following the outbreak of cable television and during the golden age of music videos. The stratospheric success of "Billie Jean" and "Beat It," his industry-saving singles, provided convincing evidence of the new technology's power to elevate an artist's image and career.

But it was just a teasing hint of the breakthroughs to come. Kerouac stalked the Negro streets wishing to be black while having little idea what that might encompass or require. But he had excuses afforded by infrequent exposure to blackness in any of its myriad forms, either up close or via popular culture.

If he were part of the Millennial Generation, he'd have blackness beamed into his house 24/7 via wireless transmission and fiber-optic cable. It would be pumping out of the booming system in his car, zipping digitally into his ears and eyes by way of iPod, Xbox, cable box, or smartphone. He could dance to it, rap with it, or sleep with it, depending on the circumstances. The multiple media platforms available to modern consumers mean that the average pair of eyeballs can absorb more demeaning images than ever before. But they also provide access to a glorious abundance of positive images. Today's nonblack consumers—especially the younger ones—are less confused by the seemingly endless datastream in which we are currently floating. They can distinguish India.Arie from Lil' Kim. They know that

Don Cheadle and Flava Flav have little in common besides skin color. More than ever, white kids know, as Langston Hughes put it, that the tom-tom laughs and the tom-tom cries.

Meanwhile, the concept of cool has successfully endured. It suffered through blaxploitation films, Quentin Tarantino movies, malt liquor commercials, and various Madison Avenue reimaginings before being revived in recent years by Denzel Washington, Michael Jordan, Usher, and others. Somehow, miraculously, cool became a part of the lingo that has never left us. And poised to benefit from these dual developments and emerge as the modern embodiment of cool was Barack Obama.

His apparently unruffled nature contributes to this widespread perception. So imperturbable is his public expression that whether he finds this amusing or perplexing is not easily determined. It must be rewarding on an emotional level, though, for someone who as an uncertain teen "tried my best to be cool at all times."

It no doubt paid off in votes and campaign donations as well. "Classy, cool, hip, glamorous, even sexy—all these words have been used to describe the presumptive Democratic nominee," the novelist Claire Messud wrote in *Newsweek* last September. She went on to confess that "even I, for the first time in my life, had given money to a campaign—his."

Novelist Paul Beatty also took note of what he calls

Obama's "jazz man equipoise." "Barack has more going for him than good timing, the proper complexion, and the appearance of marital fidelity," he noted in the *New Republic*. "He's got cool, and cool is the ultimate transcendent."

I'm reminded of an episode described by Larissa MacFarquhar in her May 2007 *New Yorker* profile of Obama. She recalls a conversation between Obama and an Illinois farmer in which the senator, not yet a candidate for the presidency, launched into an off-the-cuff description of ethanol production that sounded like it belonged in the pages of *Modern Farmer*. "Right now cellulosic ethanol is potentially eight times more energy-efficient than corn-based ethanol, because you eliminate the middle step of converting it into sugar before you convert it into ethanol," Obama explains to this farmer who has spent a lifetime up to his eyebrows in corn. That Obama's penchant for policy-wonk, chemistry-club conversation has not diluted his coolness suggests that he is returning to cool a layer of brainpower that it has lacked in recent years. Like the cosmopolitan worldview adopted by the masters of cool jazz and hard bop, or like the earlier, silk-robe savoir faire favored by Duke Ellington, Obama's brand of braininess makes one think that cool not only doesn't conflict with smarts but can no longer exist without it.

It's that element of savvy intelligence that distinguishes him from the other luminaries included in *Ebony* magazine's August 2008 feature identifying "the 25 Coolest Brothers of

All Time." Among such notables as Prince, Miles Davis, and Jimi Hendrix, perhaps only Malcolm X regularly displayed the detailed command of issues—the grandiose and the arcane—that Obama appears capable of demonstrating at any time. Not even Adam Clayton Powell, the only other elected official included, displayed such a nimble mind. In a first for the magazine, *Ebony* printed eight different covers for the issue. In addition to Obama, covers were dedicated to Prince, Jay-Z, Samuel L. Jackson, Denzel Washington, Billy Dee Williams, Marvin Gaye, and Muhammad Ali. With the possible exception of Williams, the cover honorees have all played a role in keeping the concept of black cool alive in mainstream culture.

"These brothers radiate confidence and have an alluring charisma that sets the standard," *Ebony* declared. "From their sleek, debonair styles to their smooth-as-silk personas, these magnificent Black men have conveyed, captured and conquered the quintessence of 'cool' while making it appear effortless."

On Obama's cover, he is shown emerging from a car, impeccably dressed as usual, hair freshly trimmed, eyes hidden by stylish shades. Unsmiling, his thoughts apparently aimed at some distant horizon, he exudes self-assurance. He could be a college professor, a jazz musician, the leader of the free world. He appears to possess the special knowledge that Ralph Ellison spoke of, the secret of how to make life swing.

In popularizing the idea that intelligence can be sexy, Obama's emergence presents residual benefits for black culture. The *Ebony* cover and his inclusion alongside movie stars and pop singers may lead some to consider that scholastic accomplishment is at least as attractive as "street cred" and worthy of pursuing. Could the day be far off when an African American boy has a poster of Obama (or some other intellectual) on his wall instead of one featuring the latest dropout turned NBA millionaire? One can hope, and, as Obama is fond of saying, there's nothing false about hope.

Obama's cool image has also won him admirers in the hip-hop world—a place where many politicians fear to tread. They include Jay-Z, the best-selling rapper also featured in *Ebony*'s Coolest 25. Some time ago, Jay-Z dropped stereotypical hip-hop gear and began to dress like the multi-platform media mogul he is. He now gets as much publicity for his various business projects as he does for his extremely successful music efforts.

Whereas some folks my age (forty-six) might be more inclined to see parallels between Obama's style and Adam Clayton Powell's, younger people have no trouble thinking of Jay-Z and Obama in similar terms. David J. Walker, a twenty-three-year-old student who helped organize an Obama appearance at Bowie State University in November 2006, told me the crowd was electrified when Obama entered the campus field house—and the analogy he chose was revelatory.

"When they saw him come out there, I swear I thought I was going to lose my hearing," he recalled. "You would have thought Beyoncé and Jay-Z had come in—I mean, he had that quality. In 2006 he had that quality."

Try as I might, I had difficulty mentioning Obama and Jay-Z in the same sentence. I say that not to disparage Jay-Z but simply to say that I didn't see the parallels. After looking at certain cultural developments, I no longer find it far-fetched to compare a political intellectual with a pop performer of any kind. Even so, Obama and Jay-Z seem to have no more in common than apples and oranges do.

Jay-Z, who offered vocal support of Obama during stops on his 2007 concert tour, acknowledged that others might have similar reservations. He told *Vibe* magazine, "So in the concert, I always say, 'This is not sponsored by Obama.' I make it very clear to say that, 'cause I know—'Obama associated with this guy from f——in' Marcy projects?!' I know that's coming any day. I think about that often. I mean, what do you do? What do I do? I have to support the guy. . . . But I don't wanna hurt him. I ain't like the preachers and all those guys. I don't wanna make the inappropriate statements and keep going. I'm the guy that will fall back."

If Obama saw the connection, and he often implied that he did, he showed few signs of discomfort. During the campaign for the Democratic nomination, an Obama spokesperson confirmed that Jay-Z was among the artists whose songs were on Obama's iPod. Jay-Z and his wife, Beyoncé, appeared at a number of Obama fund-raisers. So it should have come as no surprise when Obama appropriated a Jay-Z gesture in remarks following a contentious debate with Hillary Clinton. Discussing Clinton's attacks, Obama brushed his shoulders and suggested that sometimes you just have to shake 'em off. Most of the press missed the allusion, but the *Washington Post*'s Teresa Wiltz was among the first to trace it to its source, Jay-Z's 2003 hit "Dirt Off Your Shoulder." Citing Urban Dictionary, a website, she wrote that to brush one's shoulders is to begin "shaking them haters off. In other words, it means to brush off negative energy of statements made about you." Wiltz called it a "seminal moment in the campaign, the merging of politics and pop culture."

YouTube video mashups sprouted like mushrooms in cyberspace, and the shoulder brush just extended Obama's brand further into reaches where no presidential candidate had ever gone. Paul Beatty recalled seeing the gesture: " 'That was cool,' I thought. I bet the dude knows how many chambers there are in the Wu-Tang."

It's unclear whether any of the Wu-Tang Clan's extensive repertoire is also on Obama's iPod. But the clear message coming from many rap artists leading up to the election was one of unqualified support. "What [Obama] represents is, we as a people are a part of the American Dream," Jay-Z said. "The message is for a kid from Marcy projects right now to say, 'Maybe I can be the president.'" Nas, Jay-Z's onetime rival and a rapper not known for his enthusiastic support of electoral politics, also weighed in. The chorus of his song "Black President" incorporated Obama's "yes we can" mantra, while his lyrics concluded, "I'm thinkin' I can trust this brotha."

"Barack can help cure the country," he told MTV news last year. "Not just [for] us blacks, but also with all Americans. . . . Obama seems like a human being. I say that because a lot of presidents don't seem like human beings. They seem like straight-up businessmen who care about nothing but the business."

Big Boi, one-half of Outkast, a Grammy-winning duo from Atlanta, presented a compelling slice of working-class life in a music video dedicated to Obama. In "Something's Gotta Give," Big Boi rapped about trying to find "a righteous path" while inviting strangers he met on the street to volunteer at an Obama campaign office. His recruits included a distressed single mother, a young man contemplating robbing a bank, and a rootless ex-felon—not the kinds of folks who receive much help or attention from people in power. Throughout, backup vocalist Mary J. Blige pleaded with Capitol Hill while promising "in November I'll be cheering for Obama."

Over the course of the campaign, Obama made a point of telling young people, as he did at Bowie State, "You don't vote for somebody because of what they look like. You vote for somebody because of what they stand for."

At first glance, Young Jeezy, another Atlanta-based rapper, with his drug-dealing past and criminal record, doesn't seem like someone who would pay much attention to a candidate's campaign speeches. On the other hand, Jeezy opened his home to displaced survivors of Hurricane Katrina, a response from which our overmatched federal government surely benefited.

His comments before the election fell right in line with Obama's. "I'm not endorsing the dude because he's black," Young Jeezy told MTV News. "Listen to what he's saying: He's saying what I wanna hear. . . . I'mma go vote for him. I can vote, by the way. Watch me, I'm going to register to vote."

His song "My President" included what was probably the earthiest rendition of Obama's signature phrase. "We ready for damn change," Jeezy declared, "so y'all let the man shine."

Despite the occasional misfire, such as Ludacris's mixtape wishing paralysis on John McCain, the hip-hop community was overwhelmingly supportive of Obama's campaign. Undoubtedly artists and fans were responding to the candidate's message of change, as did Will.i.am, for example. But in a subculture that values cool, Obama's perceived hipness could not have hurt.

Nor did it hurt in any other quarters, except in the offices of John McCain. Frustrated by their opponent's magnetism, McCain's handlers issued a series of negative ads poking fun at the large crowds that flocked to attend Obama's speeches. According to the inscrutable logic of McCain's advisers, it was quite all right for singers to perform before packed stadiums and concert halls; that political figures would dare to do so signaled the end of civilization as we know it. Obama was neither a leader nor a statesman, the ads contended. He was something much worse: a celebrity. The ads accomplished little other than indicating the degree of desperation and confusion coming from the Republican camp. Like the shoulder brushing and fist bumps that so befuddled them earlier, the idea of a genuinely popular politician left them bewitched, bothered, and bewildered.

Actually, as we have seen, the music-biz analogies were not so far off. In hitting the right notes, in paying careful tribute to both the tragedy and the beauty of the past, in winning the respect and admiration of millions without plucking a string or touching a key, in leading a harmonious challenge against a chorus of cynics, Obama led his campaign with as much glamour, flash—and coolness—as any pop star. He not only showed the world how to sing but also demonstrated a new and hopeful way to raise our voices.

Unconvinced, Republicans ridiculed the staging of Obama's convention speech at Denver's Invesco Field. To them, the venue seemed more fitting for an athletic event or concert, the backdrop more suitable for a coronation than a speech. The public disagreed. More than 40 million viewers tuned in, a record for convention viewership. Within twenty-four hours, another three hundred thousand viewers had watched the speech on YouTube. Not surprisingly, Obama scored well with black viewers as well. Only one African American public figure has achieved higher ratings among black viewers in this decade: Michael Jackson.

CHAPTER 2
Love and Basketball

AT 3 A.M., a phone rings. Hillary Clinton answers. It's Barack Obama, calling from the White House. Apparently he's been elected president only to discover he's woefully unqualified for the job. He tells Clinton that Iran has double-crossed him, leaving him in a "blind, unreasonable, and inexperienced panic." The scene, aired on *Saturday Night Live,* wasn't the first to feature actor Fred Armisen as Obama. Nor was it the first to make fun of him. And, like the others, it provoked a hostile reaction from his supporters.

Jim Downey, the show's chief political writer, shrugged

off the complaints. He said most of the staff writers were Obama supporters. The head writer, Seth Myers, had even donated a thousand dollars to the campaign. "I would imagine that most of the comedy world is for Obama," Downey said. His statement was quite likely true, but it didn't alleviate the concerns of pro-Obama viewers. Their reaction to the skits offered prime evidence of his backers' desire to protect his image. Apparently, all was fair in comedy—unless Obama was involved.

But the response to the *SNL* skits was mild compared with the uproar surrounding the July 21 issue of the *New Yorker*. Its cover featured a cartoon depicting a newly elected Obama in the Oval Office. He was shown dressed in a costume with vague Islamic stylings. Beside him stood Michelle, garbed in camo pants and combat boots, sporting an Afro and a sash made of bullets. An assault weapon strapped to her back, she exchanged fist bumps with her husband while an American flag burned in a nearby fireplace. A portrait of Osama bin Laden smiled (or glared?) from an adjacent wall.

David Remnick, editor of the *New Yorker,* appeared baffled by the protests. "It's clearly a joke," he said, "a parody of these crazy fears and rumors and scare tactics about Obama's past and ideology. And if you can't tell it's a joke by the flag burning in the Oval Office, I don't know what more to say."

Obama's campaign staff was happy to fill in. "The *New*

Yorker may think that their cover is a satirical lampoon of the caricature Senator Obama's rightwing critics have tried to create," it said in a statement. "But most readers will see it as tasteless and offensive. And we agree."

Remnick found more to say on HuffingtonPost.com. "I wouldn't have run a cover just to get attention," he said. "The idea that we would publish a cover saying these things literally, I think, is just not in the vocabulary of what we do and who we are." The irony wasn't lost on observers who noticed Remnick issuing a defense of his publication's reputation while dismissing concerns of those doing their utmost to protect Obama's.

Not everyone was offended. Clarence Page, a Pulitzer-winning columnist and an African American, considered the cover an acceptable way to generate buzz. "It's discussion," he said on CNN's *Reliable Sources*. "It's talk. And that's what covers are supposed to do."

William Thompson, New York City's comptroller and top black elected official, had quite a different reaction. "I think it plays to every worst stereotype that's been thrown out there before," he said. "One would hope that people are bigger than that and understand that it's just an insulting cover."

A send-up of efforts to smear Obama and a deliberate attempt to do so are two distinct things, Remnick contended. He seemed confident that Americans—or his readers, at least—would know the difference. He was probably right about his readers, which would be fine if the *New Yorker* were published in a vacuum. On newsstands and in cyberspace, whatever ironic distance Remnick was counting on was certain to evaporate in a flash—and it did.

In the *Washington Post,* cultural critic Philip Kennicott wrote that the Obama team's denunciation of the cover put them "on the high ground of victimization, defensively crouched against credulous souls misreading the *New Yorker* in coal mines, truck stops and smoky saloons." What he didn't say was that the Internet had effectively replaced those conventional symbols of unlettered sentiment; items get forwarded, posted, and misconstrued with such speed and frequency that their original intent and context are quickly left behind. The user comments following articles about the controversy spelled out the potential for distortion in stark terms.

"Leave it to NYC to 'ahem' uncover the truth about Obama. Well done. Thank you," wrote a visitor to the *Los Angeles Times* website. "Truth usually does hurt!!!!!" noted an online reader of the New York *Daily News.* "Yes, it's tasteless and offensive, but there might be some truth to it too. . . . This cartoon shows an improbable, but not impossible, interpretation of the real Barack and Michelle Obama." And on the *Washington Post* website: "Finally! A candid family photo. Clever Michelle—hid them horns with your fro."

Obama said he'd seen and heard worse. But, he added,

"in attempting to satirize something, they probably fueled some misconceptions about me instead."

The misconceptions, propelled both by ignorant citizens and other, far more sophisticated Obama opponents, take on an added level (or two or three) of contention when filtered through the prism of race. That's why some African Americans in particular were less disturbed by *SNL's* humorous digs at Obama than by the casting of Armisen in the role. In truth, Armisen's complexion is not substantially different from Obama's and little was done to darken his skin. Armisen said he wore a shade of makeup known as Honey, "something I would wear when I play Prince." Described in the press as having German, Venezuelan, and Japanese heritage, Armisen could have argued that, as a living example of a multiracial union, he is ideally suited to portray Obama. (In addition, Armisen bears the distinction of being known for his impression of not one but two of the 25 Coolest Brothers Ever.) Although Armisen's portrayal of Prince and Obama is clearly affectionate, his boss, Lorne Michaels, has felt a need to defend the impersonations. About the Obama character, he said that Armisen won the part in an open competition. "It's not about race," he told the *Washington Post*. "It's about getting a take on Obama, where it serves the comedy and the writing." He once told the *New York Times,* "there's nothing mocking or critical about the way Fred does Prince. You can tell that he paid attention in that kind of detail to Prince because he admired him that much. He comes from the place of a fan."

Clearly Michaels, a veteran of show business, knows that the line between love and theft is sometimes so fragile it's lost in the glare of the stage lights. His defensive testimonies—and the compulsion to express them—stem from blackface's long association with racism. That Armisen wears Honey instead of shoe polish doesn't get him a free pass, whether he deserves one or not.

"The blackface mask is utterly taboo, in a way no other comic impersonations of ethnicity or identity are," writes John Strausbaugh in *Black Like You: Blackface, Whiteface, Insult and Imitation in American Popular Culture*. Gwendolyn C. Jackson, a criminal defense attorney and an African American, told Fox News, "We want to make sure [Obama] is not derailed in any way, and most important, he's not portrayed in a very negative light. . . . Anytime you start darkening up or blackening up an actor, a lot of people start thinking about minstrels."

But, as Paul Farhi pointed out in the *Washington Post*, *SNL* cast member Darrell Hammond has worn lightly colored makeup to impersonate Jesse Jackson for years, and decades ago Billy Crystal did the same while playing Sammy Davis Jr. So why didn't blacks object then?

In fact, *SNL* has been harder on Jackson, a former guest host, than it has been on Obama. "The Obama Files," a cartoon sketch that first ran during the Democratic primaries, depicted him and Al Sharpton as simpletons in the extreme and aired without comment. In contrast, when actors made fun of Rosa Parks in *Barbershop,* a 2002 film starring Ice Cube, Jackson and Sharpton were among the first to raise objections. Perhaps no one felt as compelled to come to Jackson's defense because he has lapsed from relevance and into unwitting self-parody. Sammy Davis Jr., despite being named to *Ebony*'s "coolest" list, vanished from most African Americans' radar screens after he infamously embraced Richard Nixon way back in 1972. As the current symbol of both black dignity and black ambition, Obama presents a new and stimulating challenge for would-be guardians of African American identity.

The risk of *SNL*'s alternate take on nontraditional casting even caught the eye of critics overseas. Writing in the *Guardian,* a British newspaper, Hannah Pool argued, "Casting a black actor wouldn't have guaranteed the quality of the sketch, but it would have made the whole thing a lot less shoddy. Let's get one thing straight. The moment anyone starts reaching for 'blackface,' they are on extremely dodgy territory. Anyone who thinks it's necessary or, for that matter, remotely funny to black-up needs to have the gauge on their moral compass reset."

Pool's argument about necessity intrigues me. Was it necessary to darken Armisen's skin? Editorial cartoonists, especially the skilled ones, are able to suggest Obama's identity by exaggerating a few characteristics; they seldom darken or even crosshatch his skin. Like the *New Yorker*'s target readers, isn't *SNL*'s audience sufficiently attuned to satire by now to get the joke without the makeup?

Behind the hand-wringing is the inescapable worry that whites still fail when attempting to determine the genuine identity of black individuals, that somehow, like layers of lampblack, myths and misconceptions obscure the real human beings beneath it all. Throughout Obama's campaign, African Americans were frustrated by white voters' complaints that they "still didn't know who he was and what he stood for." In such a setting, anything that threatens clarity sets off alarms.

"Only a handful of words and symbols have been considered absolutely taboo in current American society, unreservedly banned and forbidden," John Strausbaugh has written. "The swastika is one. The word 'nigger,' uttered by anyone not black, is another. Blackface is a third." Despite this, white Americans continue to display a strange compulsion to blacken their faces. Even some Millennials, who, as we have seen, are far less hung up about race than are others, occasionally darken their skin and act out bizarre rituals of stereotype and dysfunction.

I remember being an undergraduate on the campus of Northwestern University and watching, appalled, as members of a prominent white fraternity marched along the main avenue in blackface and grass skirts. More than twenty years later, reports of campus blackface parties began to circulate when photos of such gatherings appeared on the Internet. The images included a scene at a Clemson party in which students dressed in what they believed to be gang gear while displaying blackface paint and padded buttocks.

According to the *Los Angeles Times,* "gangsta"-themed parties have been held on campuses "from Connecticut to Colorado." Strausbaugh lists several universities where such events took place between 2000 and 2005, including Georgia State, Penn State, the University of Nebraska, and the University of Virginia. Students have attended as blackface versions of such well-known African Americans as Charles Barkley, Tiger Woods, Venus and Serena Williams, Clarence Thomas, and Anita Hill.

The *Los Angeles Times* quoted a black academic who reserved his ire for black rap performers who perpetuate stereotypes. They should be blamed for the parties, he suggested, because their antics leave white kids "kind of confused." His pat rationale conveniently overlooks whites' long fascination with blackening up, a tradition that far precedes gangsta rap.

As Strausbaugh points out, it also precedes minstrel shows (although they must be blamed for popularizing it). He writes, "Although it was certainly racist, it was sometimes something other than that, a reflection of the complex of neuroses and pathologies that mark relations between whites and blacks in America—a complicated web of love and hate, fear and guilt, attraction and repulsion, mockery and mimicry."

It's somewhat dispiriting that mockery and mimicry can never be just that—a sketch can never be just a sketch, an impersonation simply an impersonation—where American performance is concerned. Obama would be the first to proclaim the necessity of leaving some aspects of history behind, but blackface seems too magnetic and controversial for either blacks or whites to completely abandon it.

Its tentacles are in too deep. It may have peaked in the mid-1800s, but it didn't exactly disappear after that. In 1927, about a hundred years after white performer George Washington Dixon attained stardom singing "Zip Coon" and became one of the most notorious blackface characters ever, Al Jolson appeared onscreen in *The Jazz Singer,* America's first film with spoken dialogue.

Jolson starred as Jack Robin, formerly Jakie Rabinowitz from "the New York ghetto." Although he comes from a long line of talented cantors, Jack chooses jazz instead. He runs away from home and becomes an entertainer. Finally back in New York and on the cusp of stardom, Jack resists the pull of family and synagogue as he prepares for his Broadway debut. In the "New York ghetto," the unspoken question is whether Jack remains "Jewish enough." As the Day of Atonement approaches, Jack blacks up to rehearse his debut number. "I'd love to sing for my people," he tells his love interest, "but I belong here."

But the smell of the greasepaint and the roar of the crowd aren't in the end strong enough to hold his attention. "There's something after all, in my heart," he confesses, "the cry of my race." Because he's in full blackface when he discloses this, the irony is profound. When he stares at his darkened face in the mirror and sees the face of his father gazing back, he is forced to acknowledge who he really is. He takes off his wig of matted hair and weeps.

That scene is closely echoed in *Tropic Thunder,* a blackface film released last August. Like Jolson, a blackened-up and emotional Robert Downey Jr. declares, "I know who I am," removes his matted wig, and confronts his true, genuine self. Through the artifice of blackness, Jolson and Downey arrive at hard-won authenticity. Without blackness as a barometer and mirror by which they can bare their souls, they live in a state of emotional and professional paralysis, hiding—unfulfilled—behind their art.

Downey plays Kirk Lazarus, an Australian five-time Oscar winner who gets way too immersed in his characters. In the movie within the movie (also called *Tropic Thunder*), he's Lincoln Osyrus, a tough black soldier with a heart of gold. Before the movie goes into production, Lazarus undergoes a "pigmentation alteration procedure" that darkens his skin. On-set, he's challenged by rapper-actor Alpa Chino (Brandon T. Jackson), playing a streetwise black soldier named Brooklyn. Chino says he took the part because "I just knew I had to represent. Because they had one good part for a black man and they gave it to Crocodile Dundee." Chino has unwittingly taken up the banner for Richard Wright, who described the relationship between blacks and whites as a battle over the nature of reality.

Finally fed up, Chino calls Lazarus a "koala-huggin' nigga." A scuffle ensues, during which Lazarus lectures, "for four hundred years, that word has kept us down." He segues into the theme song of *The Jeffersons,* reciting the lyrics as a heartfelt monologue.

"At first I was like kinda weird about it," Jackson told reelblack.com when asked about working with Downey in blackface. "At the same time, when I saw him playing the role, I said, 'Okay, this dude is a beast.' Being a black actor like that, he became a black man. He didn't really like be in blackface. He really actually became black."

Jackson said Downey's method acting continued long after the director ended a scene. "He'd still be going. He'd be like, 'I'ma go to the trailer and get me some barbecue ribs and some chicken and some barbecue sauce. You want to go with me, Brandon?' I'd be like, what the hell is this? Dude was being very committed, you know what I mean?"

Inexplicably—or perhaps not—Jackson pointed to Obama as a way for viewers to resolve any conflicting reactions to Downey's performance. "If you still have an issue then, I mean, there's a lot of issues we can have," he said. "Get some money and get these gas prices, man. . . . Vote for Barack if you gon' have issues. So, Obama!"

White critics tended to give Downey a pass, pointing to Jackson's character as a built-in foil that effectively counters any notions of minstrelsy or stereotyping. In the *New York Times,* Manohla Dargis called Downey's black soldier, who speaks in a strange pastiche of broken English and moldy slang, "the most recognizably human character in a lampoon rife with caricatures." She considered the use of blackface "softer . . . compared with the rather more vulgar and far less loving exploitation of what you might call Jewface." Slate critic Dana Stevens commented, "There are a lot of things you could say about Robert Downey Jr.'s portrayal of a white man playing a black man in this movie, but 'unoriginal' is hardly one of them."

Most baffling was David Edelstein's review in *New York* magazine. He loved Downey's performance, in which the actor "respects the beauty and weight and potency of the archetype. He drops his voice an octave (at least) and what comes out is gorgeous. He really does make a damn fine Negro." Edelstein may have been employing the same kind of insider's irony that the *New Yorker* cover aimed for, but if so, he, too, missed the mark. Downey's character "craves authenticity so deeply," he wrote, "that you want to believe he's a black actor playing a black soldier." That Downey, for all his craving, never comes close to anything near authenticity, passes without remark.

Much like black people's own obsession with "keeping it real," some whites seem to desire some imaginary version of spiritual purity from black people in order to arrive at a clearer picture of reality. As David Gates put it in a *Newsweek* essay, "ever since there were black Americans, whites have tended to hear in their music an authenticity presumably unavailable to the overcivilized." It has never been just music. John Howard Griffin, author of *Black Like Me,* said it like this: "How else except by becoming a Negro could a white man hope to know the truth?"

While neither Gates nor Griffin is guilty of this, they hint at the complex love-hate dynamic that long defined whites' attitude toward blacks. They love the window into truth that blackness allegedly provides while caring little for blacks as people. It's a thin line between such strong emotions, and that line forms yet another strand of the tightrope that Obama has traversed with daring and skill.

Clay Cane, an African American film critic, lauded Downey for convincingly playing "a white guy who can convincingly play black." (See how the film's movie-within-a-movie effectively insulates it from criticism? For instance, it's easy to sidestep my comments about Downey's unconvincing "black" speech by saying, "It wasn't Downey's choice. It was a choice made by 'Kirk Lazarus.' His choosing poorly only proves the brilliance of Downey's performance." Et cetera.) Although Cane insisted that "Downey's Negro voice and blackedy-black jokes were grating," he somehow found it all "pure, funny, and void of racism."

Downey reportedly said of his role, "If it's done right, it could be the type of role you called Peter Sellers to do 35

years ago. If you don't do it right, we're going to hell." To
which, Jasmyne Cannick, an African American who writes
frequently about popular culture, replied, "Note to Downey:
Do not pass go. Do not collect $200 million. Go straight to
hell where Satan is anxiously awaiting your arrival."

Cannick's reaction comes closer to the opinions I found
among African Americans. They were flustered by an
America that can respond to calls for moving beyond race
while helping a movie that thrives on African American
and Jewish stereotypes to gross just under $100 million after
four weekends in theaters.

It's these conflicting impulses—affection and con-
tempt—that arouse skepticism in African Americans, even
those trying mightily to answer Obama's call for enlight-
ened optimism.

The creators of *Tropic Thunder* dodged complaints
about the movie by employing the kind of lingo that their
own script viciously parodies. Cowriter Justin Theroux told
Variety, "We were just careful to always keep the humor
where it belongs, which is on the lunacy of Hollywood and
the way things are cast and the fact that that guy could get
that role even today, as Laurence Olivier did when he played
'Othello.'" Once you get past Theroux's galling mention of
his script in the same sentence as a work of Shakespeare,
you can see his point, sort of. How else could a talented
German-Japanese-Venezuelan be cast as the first Kenyan-
Kansan-American to win his party's nomination for president?

Since Theroux mentioned Olivier, I can't help wondering what the great thespian would have thought of Downey's performance. He hesitated to play the jealous Moor for years, daunted by "the difficulties of creating the voice and characteristics of Othello." Like Downey, he appears to have lowered his voice an octave or two when he finally took on the part. Unfortunately, though, when Olivier recites, "Haply, for I am black, / And have not those soft parts of conversation / That chamberers have," he looks less black than burned—ashen, ghoulish even. In truth, he looks less like a Moor than like Alan Cumming as Nightcrawler in *X2*. Despite Olivier's respectful, committed performance, his bizarre appearance is a distraction. Once again, an earnest attempt to get at the alleged mystery of black identity gets smudged.

Just as Olivier's acting had no hint of parody, neither did that of John Howard Griffin. In the fall of 1959, Griffin shaved his head and darkened his skin with the aid of chemicals and a sunlamp. His purpose? "To enter the world of the Negro," to learn "what it is like to be a Negro in a land where we keep the Negro down."

In photos of Griffin in disguise, his makeup looks no more convincing than Olivier's. Nonetheless, his effort was dogged and courageous, albeit hampered by a tendency to dwell on the most somber aspects of black existence in the 1950s. Where Kerouac heard life, joy, kicks, and music, Griffin heard only the blues. Whereas blackness was for

Kerouac a source of mystery, wonder, and perhaps titilla-
tion, for Griffin it was an endless font of despair, frustration, and pain. Whatever joy and gratitude he encountered
among poor blacks in Louisiana, Mississippi, Alabama, and
Georgia was all too often seen not as genuine feeling but as
symptoms of a view of reality warped and twisted by the
ravages of racism.

One night, as the guest of a poor laborer, his wife, and
their six children, Griffin paused before drifting to sleep on
their shanty floor. "Odors of the night and autumn and the
swamp entered to mingle with the inside odors of children,
kerosene, cold beans, urine, and the dead incense of pine
ashes," he wrote. "The rots and the freshness combined into
a strange fragrance—the smell of poverty. For a moment I
knew the intimate and subtle joys of misery." In scenes like
these, he came perilously close to wringing the erotic from
black suffering.

Speaking as a "black" man, he noted that white men
and women "could not see me or any other black man as
a human individual because they buried us under the gar-
bage of their stereotyped view of us." One aspect of that
stereotype is the hapless victim, and it's a note that Griffin
struck often. In his defense, he acknowledged that his brief
(six weeks') foray, recalled in *Black Like Me,* could only shed
so much light. "To get from the white world into the Negro
world is a complex matter," he wrote.

These days, for many African Americans, success

depends on getting from the "black world" to the white. Doing so while hanging on to whatever aspects of black identity we decide are worth keeping defines our existential dilemma. Obama's ability to bridge these worlds with minimal visible angst fascinates and inspires us. According to Obama, the bridge is constructed from and strengthened by "a constant cross-pollination among people and cultures." From the transference emerges a new world neither black nor white but enriched by all it contains. The identities that Griffin found so hidebound are now, in Obama's view, "scrambling, and then cohering in new ways. Beliefs keep slipping through the noose of predictability."

But before he arrived at such conclusions, he needed to know more about blackness than his mirror could tell him. "I was trying to raise myself to be a black man in America," he recalled in his memoir. "And beyond the given of my appearance, no one around me seemed to know exactly what that meant." As a part of his youthful, seventies-era explorations of black identity, Obama began to play basketball. Without necessarily intending to, he developed a love of the game.

"He didn't know who he was until he found basketball," his brother-in-law Craig Robinson has said. "It was the first time he really met black people."

Basketball, as much as anything, helped challenge conventional notions of black masculinity in particular. Obama told Bryant Gumbel, "Growing up in Hawaii without a father, without a large African American population, here is a place where being black was not a disadvantage. Here is a sport in which we were dominant. All those things contributed to the idea that there was something special about it."

In interviews, his high school teammates have said that nothing about Obama's behavior suggested that he was struggling to fit in. "He never let that show, so maybe it was more of an internal struggle," one of them told ABC News.

Keeping it to himself—and developing his famous unruffled nature—became part of the black male identity that he was trying on for size. Like so many of us in his generation, he chose famous basketball players to study and imitate.

He told Gumbel, "As a fan, back in the mid and late seventies, there were a lot of cool basketball players. Dr. J. Walt Frazier." Back then, a poster of Julius "Dr. J." Erving, soaring in for a dunk, graced Obama's bedroom wall. (His white friends idolized Erving, too. "Seemed like half of 'em wanted to be black themselves—or at least Dr. J.," he recalled in *Dreams from My Father*.) Just as the Blue Note album covers of the forties, fifties, and sixties helped usher in the very notion of cool, posters of Walt "Clyde" Frazier, Erving, and others helped redefine cool and sustain it through the seventies.

Instead of hipster shades and sleek suits, the icons of cool now sported skyscraping Afros and matching muttonchops.

Obama has noticed similar parallels. "There's something about basketball and our culture that connects up with the African American experience in a special way, almost in the same way that jazz music connects up with African American culture. There's an aspect of improvisation within a discipline that I find very powerful."

As Frazier sees it, cool itself is a form of discipline. "Cool is a quality admired in the black neighborhoods," he once explained. "Cool is a matter of self-preservation, of survival. It must go back to the slave days, when oftentimes all a black man had to defend himself with was his poise. If you'd show fear or anger, you'd suffer the consequences. Today, the guy respected in the ghetto is the guy who resists the urge to go off—who can handle himself in a crisis, who can talk his way out of a fight."

Finding his way in Hawaii, Obama took such notions to heart.

As a member of his school's state champion basketball team his senior year, Obama wore the number 23. Coincidentally, another number 23's trailblazing cultural influence helped pave the way for Obama's eventual emergence: Michael Jordan, who, until the advent of Tiger Woods, had long been the most recognized athlete on the planet. According to the *Los Angeles Times,* "the roots of the Jordan phenomenon" can be traced to Erving, whose elegant, graceful image watched over young Barack Obama while he slept. Dr. J., the paper noted, drew "attention to a relatively young and decidedly second-class league." By the time Jordan was done, the NBA was widely considered one of the most successful sports enterprises ever—and Jordan accounted for an estimated 10 to 20 percent of its annual revenue.

A 1998 *Forbes* article on "the Jordan effect" estimated that he had generated $10 billion since joining the league in 1984. That total included his commercials for Nike athletic wear, Hanes underwear, Coca-Cola, an upscale men's fragrance, one movie, *Space Jam,* and more than seventy books written by and about him. Advertisers were eager to sign him up because of his power to charm audiences of every background.

"He transcends the sport of basketball," enthused a Nike exec in an article in *Hoop* magazine. "He transcends almost every kind of category you could put him in," a sports marketing expert added. We didn't hear that much talk of "transcendence" again until Obama shot out of relative obscurity to challenge the Clintons for Democratic dominance. A bridge-builder with brawn and charisma to spare, Jordan displayed an off-court demeanor that was confident and easygoing. Anyone could see it from almost any distance: he was cool.

But he was not the first black superpitchman. That distinction belongs to Bill Cosby.

According to WalletPop, a personal-finance website produced by AOL.com, the top twenty-five celebrity spokespersons of all time include four black men (no black women made the list). Along with James Earl Jones (former pitchman for Verizon) and O. J. Simpson (for his Hertz ads; who can forget those?), Jordan was ranked No. 4 and Cosby was No. 1. In ads for Jell-O, Ford Motor Company, Coca-Cola, E. F. Hutton, and others, Cosby consistently scored high "Q," or likability, ratings. Mugging but never undignified, Cosby came across in ads as wise, warm, and fatherly. While hardly emasculated, his ad persona was not particularly sexual. And, although Jordan doesn't swagger in his ads, he does come off as unmistakably virile.

Jordan's success as an advertising spokesman prompted basketball writer Mark Vancil to declare, quite convincingly, "If O. J. Simpson and Arthur Ashe crossed the color line in product endorsement, Jordan obliterated it."

As heir to the cool tradition established by the preceding generation of basketball heroes, he could reach mainstream audiences longing for life, joy, kicks, and music. In *Black Planet,* his memoir about the role of race in the NBA, David Shields quotes a fan who spells out the appeal of Jordan and his peers in no uncertain terms: "For white guys, for millions of white guys including myself who are not cool!!, watching basketball is one last chance if not to be cool at least to get in contact with cool."

Jordan got hurt at the start of the 1985–1986 season (his second) but recovered in time to set a record for the most points scored in an NBA playoff game. Obama, arriving in Chicago that same year, began in a much quieter way as a community organizer on the city's South Side. "I'm glad I ended up in Chicago," Jordan has said. "I was in the right place at the right time." Over time, Obama would also come to view his adopted hometown as a place of fortuitous potential. He recalled, "As segregated as Chicago was, as strained as race relations were, the success of the civil rights movement had at least created some overlap between communities, more room to maneuver for people like me."

While Jordan has resolutely avoided politics (although he has contributed to several campaigns, including Obama's), his political prospects, should he ever entertain them, seem bright. As we have seen with Sly Stone and Jimi Hendrix, Jordan conjures visions of transracial conciliation—the same kinds of visions constantly invoked during Obama's campaign for the White House. Consider *Washington Post* columnist Michael Wilbon's comments about Jordan's impact on Chicago, written in 1998: "Jordan made us—and I am definitely including myself—feel better about ourselves and our city. This is a bolder, yet more tolerant place because he brought various peoples and cultures together—if only for two hours at a time—which is something segregated Chicago had always resisted."

A convincing example of Jordan's cultural influence can be found in Gatorade's 1992 "Be Like Mike" commercial. Backed by a lilting beat and jubilant vocals, footage of Jordan vanquishing NBA opponents is mixed with scenes of the athlete cavorting with sun-splashed Americans of various hues. As adults and children sing the virtues of moving and grooving like Mike, he moves among them as a pied piper of joy. In just sixty seconds, a vision of multiracial unity—led by a black man, no less—is vividly rendered.

Becoming temporarily dark-skinned has usually been either cathartic for white characters (in *The Jazz Singer* and *Tropic Thunder,* for example), hellish (*Black Like Me*), or comical (Gene Wilder in *Silver Streak*). In contrast, the strategic marketing of Michael Jordan, especially in commercials such as "Be Like Mike," implies that taking on the mantle of blackness is not only virtuous but pleasurable.

Geoffrey Norman, writing for *National Review*'s website, observed that "Jordan is one of those rare athletes with a blend of personality and skills that transcends the game and makes fans out of people who never cared before. What Ali did for boxing, Jordan did for basketball and Tiger Woods is doing for golf."

And, for a brief, extraordinary stretch, Obama is doing for politics.

CHAPTER 3
At the Threshold

THREE DAYS AFTER moving to Chicago to begin a job as a community organizer, Obama walked into a black barbershop. As he sat in the barber's chair and had his 'fro trimmed, he absorbed a quick primer on the career and legacy of Harold Washington. It was 1985, and Washington, Chicago's first (and only) black elected mayor, was battling a city council bitterly opposed to his reformist agenda. Listening to the various testimonies of the men in the barbershop, Obama got an inkling of the enormous potential of change, what it could accomplish and what it required. Washington had failed the first time he ran for mayor, the men told him.

The defeat had been a source of shame, as was "the lack of unity within the black community, the doubts that had to be overcome. But Harold had tried again, and this time the people were ready."

Two years earlier, Eddie Murphy had also observed Washington's activities in Chicago, although he used far saltier language to describe his conclusion. "Shit's changing," he said. "We got black politicians now." It was good of him to notice.

"Who's that boy? Harold Washington?"

Murphy was onstage at Constitution Hall in Washington, D.C. Clad in skintight red leather pants and a matching jacket unzipped nearly to the waist, Murphy correctly pointed out that Washington's victory was one of the inspirations behind Jesse Jackson's campaign for the presidency. He told the audience he'd seen Jesse in the gym working out. "I seen him running around the track. I said, 'Why the f——k you getting in shape?'"

Murphy acted out Jackson's "reply" so hilariously that it defies description. Jesse said he had to work out, Murphy explained, because he knew he'd have to make his presidential speeches while ducking and dodging the bullets that would surely be flying in his direction.

Murphy then mimed a would-be white assassin growing frustrated as he tried to center the swift Jackson in his gunsight: "He won't stand still!"

Murphy's mostly black audience laughed heartily. Not

only was Murphy funny, but he was also putting his own witty spin on the gallows humor that had already been circulating in black communities for months. In his routine, Murphy revealed how "Run, Jesse, Run!" had acquired more than one meaning.

Similar notions led Chris Rock's character in *Head of State* to spend so much time thinking about the threat of assassination. As Mays Gilliam, a Washington alderman improbably elected to the White House, Rock confronted— albeit comically—the likelihood that he would be shot in office.

The possibility has never been far from any discussion about African American candidates for the presidency. Alma Powell, wife of Colin, mentioned such fears—and the hate mail she received—amid calls for her husband to run in 1996. "You think everybody loves Colin Powell," she told a reporter from *Ladies' Home Journal*. "Everybody doesn't like Colin Powell. One day I got two letters—one telling me what a wonderful man I was married to and how much the country needed him; the other said Colin Powell is a scumbag and proceeded to list all his evils. A black man running for president is going to be in a dangerous position."

Bruce Gordon, former president of the NAACP, said he also feared for Powell when the general was weighing a run. He told the Associated Press, "when Powell decided not to run, I said to myself, 'Good,' because I thought someone would kill him. This time, I think that if, out of fear, we keep our most talented people from running for office, it will never happen. Yes, there's a risk, but I would never want it to be in the way. In running, Barack Obama has to accept the fact that he faces a risk. And, yes, we pray for him."

Rep. Bennie Thompson (D-MS), chairman of the House Homeland Security Committee, didn't want to rely solely on entreaties to the Almighty. He wrote a letter to the Secret Service to make sure that Obama was well protected. He said he did so because Obama's candidacy "is so unique to this country and so important that the last thing you would want is for him not to have the opportunity to fulfill the role of a potential presidential nominee. It's out of an abundance of caution that I wrote the letter, rather than keep our fingers crossed and pray."

So pervasive were fears for Obama's safety that they threatened to hurt his chances with some black voters. A sixty-one-year-old black hairdresser hinted to the *New York Times* that she was considering not casting a ballot for Obama in the South Carolina primary. She feared, she said, "that they would just kill him." Gilda Cobb-Hunter, a Democratic state representative in South Carolina, told the paper that she found such concerns deeply troubling. "Maybe it's a Southern thing," she said. "They want to protect him from the bad people, and in order to protect him, they won't support him. They want to see him around, making a difference."

Such sentiments, especially in African Americans old

enough to remember, derive from the assassinations of the 1960s. When I was growing up, my parents and other adults often speculated about what life would be like if King had lived, or how high Medgar Evers would have risen if he hadn't been shot down in Jackson, Mississippi. Like my parents and their friends, Representative Thompson raised the specter of our recent past. His letter said, "As an African-American who was witness to some of this nation's most shameful days during the civil rights movement, I know personally that the hatred of some of our fellow citizens can lead to heinous acts of violence. We need only to look to the assassinations of the Rev. Dr. Martin Luther King Jr. and 1968 presidential candidate Robert Kennedy as examples."

The fallout from those slayings also resonates through art and entertainment with political themes, such as Eddie Murphy's routine and Chris Rock's movie, and more dramatic offerings such as *24.* The first two seasons of Fox network's popular suspense thriller featured Dennis Haysbert as David Palmer, a black senator who eventually won the presidency. But he spent much of his campaign and his tenure in office with a target on his back. In season five, he was assassinated.

Haysbert was not pleased. He told the *Los Angeles Times,* "I was very upset. We live in this country where we have killed off all these beloved leaders—JFK, RFK, Martin Luther King. Why would you ever want to take a show that has produced a wonderful character that everyone loves and do that?"

Palmer's admirers included Sen. John McCain, who told *Entertainment Weekly* that Palmer was his favorite on-screen president. "He's fabulous," he said. "He's a guy who makes tough decisions, he takes charge, he's ready to sacrifice his interest on behalf of the country."

A similar, earlier effort, though not so well done, was *The Man,* a 1972 film based on Irving Wallace's mammoth novel of the same title. Despite being the first full-scale film treatment of a black president of the United States, it came and went comparatively quickly. (The novel, however, was on the *New York Times* best-seller list for about eight months.)

Played by James Earl Jones, Douglass Dillman is president pro tem of the Senate when the commander-in-chief and everyone else in the line of succession meet untimely deaths. Brooding and hesitant, he faces a 40 percent approval rating when he takes office. "I am a black man, not yet qualified for human being, let alone for president," he says. Dillman is under pressure from all sides, squeezed in particular by southern racists who scheme to throw him out of office and black militants who want him to pursue an aggressive pro-black agenda.

New York Times film critic Vincent Canby suggested that the production sidestepped important themes that it should have addressed head-on. "About halfway through 'The Man,'" he wrote, "one comes to realize that, in its own unwitting way, the film is much more interested in contemplating incompetence than in presenting any ideas about politics, race relations, international diplomacy, personal ambition, courage, or what-have-you."

Dillman quickly suspects that everyone is after him— and he's right. The movie's tagline says it all: "The first black president of the United States. First they swore him in. Then they swore to get him."

Few African Americans would disagree that their paranoia—or, shall we say, justifiable wariness—about such matters is fair game for artistic treatment. Who knows, it might even be the subject of a *New Yorker* cover down the line. But their tolerance is challenged—and their fears heightened—by comments in the political arena that seem to go far beyond satire and straight to the gut.

Thus the outrage (but not disbelief) when Mike Huckabee, speaking at the National Rifle Association last May and inspired by a loud noise, offered an ill-considered ad-lib. "That was Barack Obama," he said. "He just tripped off a chair. He's getting ready to speak and somebody aimed a gun at him and he—he dove for the floor." Huckabee quickly apologized for his comments, probably never realizing how closely his joke resembled Eddie Murphy's raunchier version twenty-four years before.

Thus the outrage (but not disbelief) when, less than a week later, Hillary Clinton told the Sioux Falls, South Dakota, *Argus Leader* editorial board, "My husband did not wrap up the nomination in 1992 until he won the California primary somewhere in the middle of June, right? We all remember Bobby Kennedy was assassinated in June in California. I don't understand it," Clinton said.

Thus the outrage (but not disbelief) when, less than a week after Clinton's Freudian slip, Fox contributor Liz Trotta jokingly wished for the assassination of Sen. Barack Obama. When the anchor asked her if she was talking about "knocking off" Osama or Obama, she replied, "Both, if we could." After which, a cry could be heard in living rooms across black America: What do you mean, "we"?

To many African Americans, more disturbing than the sheer bodaciousness of such comments was the probability that Huckabee, Clinton, and Trotta merely said aloud what many, many others were thinking. Maybe all of that will help explain why conspiracy theories often have startling staying power in some areas of black conversation.

One would think that after decades of diversity training and celebrations of multiculturalism, nostalgic talk of hunting and killing Negroes (and their commie-agitator friends) would be discreetly confined to private parlors. After *Roots,* after Sidney Poitier and Colin Powell, shouldn't whites know better? In truth, most of them do and consistently demonstrate it—not just in their un-precedented support for Obama but also in many areas of social and public interaction. In addition, television and movies in recent years have helped to advance the accep-tance of African Americans in leadership positions. But progress is a relatively recent development. To appreciate how far we have come, let's briefly visit the place from which we came.

The first cinematic treatment of a black chief executive was *Rufus Jones for President,* a musical short produced in 1933. The title character was winningly played by Sammy Davis Jr., just seven years old. Watching this film recently, I never got a clear sense that young Rufus was supposed to be president of *the United States.* Because this was never explicitly said, I half suspected he was presiding over a lodge meeting or a watermelon-lovers club.

After a bully reduces young Davis to tears, his mother (Ethel Waters, who got top billing) attempts to comfort him. She gathers him on her lap and tells him she foresees great things ahead.

Is I gwine be a great man, Mammy?

You sure is. You gwine be . . . president.

Me?

Sure. They has kings your age. I don't see no reason they can't have presidents. Besides, the book
says anybody born here can be president.

While comparing her son to a cloud that's "dark and dense" but has a silver lining, she advises him to stay on his "own side of the fence." Her front-porch counsel segues into a dream of a presidential campaign that her little boy wins.

Little Sammy, decked out in top hat and tux, places his hand on a telephone book and is administered the oath of office.

> Now first of all swear to me that pork chops will be free.
>
> . . . Now swear to me instead of a boost, that the tax on razors must be reduced.
>
> . . . Swear to me that you will choose for the national anthem "Memphis Blues."
>
> . . . Swear to me that watermelon vines are public property at all times.

Mammy soon appoints herself "presidentess" and introduces new laws designed to make chicken stealing and watermelon nabbing easier on the populace.

The musical numbers are outstanding, especially those led by Davis, a true prodigy, and Waters. But they are regularly interrupted by seemingly every antiblack stereotype known to man. Puns and sight gags revolve around razors, dice, and the aforementioned chicken stealing, among other gems.

But the worst scenes take place on the Senate floor. With all the eye rolling and shucking and jiving, the scenes recall those in *The Birth of a Nation* (1915) in which black legislators (actually white actors in blackface) are shown to be more concerned with eating fried chicken than passing laws.

The myth of the incompetent black lawmaker sprang from the disaffected southern imagination and continued to flourish into the twentieth century. Following Thomas Jefferson and taking up the argument that slavery had been a blessing for those taken captive, whites in power put forth the notion that blacks were incapable of self-government.

While the nation's moviemakers were churning out the likes of *The Birth of a Nation* and *Rufus Jones,* its "scholars" were doing their part. Foremost among them was Columbia University professor William Archibald Dunning. In his books and lectures, he perpetuated the idea that Reconstruction had ruined the South. For Dunning, blacks "had no pride of race and no aspiration or ideals save to be like whites." A school of historians developed from his teachings. Its members included James Ford Rhodes, who, citing the eminent niggerologist Louis Agassiz, argued against "the policy of trying to make negroes intelligent by legislative acts." Another member, John W. Burgess, wrote, "a black skin means membership in a race of men which has never of itself succeeded in subjecting passion to reason." Which explains that whole obsession with watermelon, chicken, and dice.

But the facts, of course, were different.

Before Emancipation, only two blacks are known to have held elective office. After the Civil War, however, the first trickle began. The historian Eric Foner has written, "From the army would come many of the black political leaders of Reconstruction, including at least forty-one delegates to state constitutional conventions, sixty legislators, three lieutenant governors, and four Congressmen."

In his book *Capitol Men,* the historian Philip Dray describes these trailblazing statesmen—men like Robert Smalls, Robert Brown Elliott, and John Roy Lynch—as "smart, tough, adaptable individuals—as resilient as they were resourceful." What's more, they "tended to be—had to be—exceptional individuals. . . . In general they brought an impressive degree of competence and dedication to their jobs, dispelling critics' claims that they possessed no aptitude for politics or statesmanship."

Historians such as Dunning suggested that the influx of black elected officials made the prospect of dreaded "Negro domination" possible or even likely. In truth, however, perception outweighed reality. According to Dray, during the 1880s, no more than two blacks served in Congress; "three were present for the Fifty-first Congress (1889–91), and from 1891 to 1901, no more than one participated."

Only one, Arthur Mitchell, was in Congress (1935–1943) when Jesse Owens beat the Nazis and Joe Louis knocked out Max Schmeling. Though those victories had no immediate impact on politics, they did help upgrade the image of black men in ways that even the most skilled black congressman could not. "What my father did was enable white America to think of him as an American, not a black," said his son Joe Louis Jr. "By winning, he became white America's first black hero."

Only one black congressman, the terminally quiet William L. Dawson, was in office (1943–1970) when Adam Clayton Powell arrived in 1945 and began to shake things up.

Ten years later, Powell was joined by Charles Diggs, a Democrat from Michigan. Diggs first attracted national attention in 1955, when he wrote to Judge Curtis Swango seeking permission to monitor the Emmett Till murder trial in Mississippi. In her memoir, *Death of Innocence* (written with Christopher Benson), Emmett Till's mother, Mamie Till-Mobley, recalls Diggs's arrival:

> *The judge had given his permission but somebody forgot to tell Sheriff Strider and his crew. When Diggs and a couple of associates couldn't get in the doors, the reporter Jimmy Hicks got involved and offered to take the congressman's card to the judge.*
>
> *Hicks recalled a deputy taking the card and remarking, "This nigger says that other nigger is a congressman."*
>
> *"A nigger congressman?" the second deputy exclaimed. "It ain't possible. It ain't legal."*

If the idea of a black legislator was unbelievable, a black president was inconceivable.

By 1971, when young Obama was returning to Honolulu to enroll in fifth grade, Diggs had become chairman of the first Congressional Black Caucus. There were thirteen charter members in all and more than fourteen hundred black elected officials across the country. That number included Carl Stokes, who in 1967 became the first black mayor of a major city (Cleveland, Ohio). The fanciful was becoming real.

In March 1972, the first National Black Political Convention brought four thousand activists to Gary, Indiana, where the city's black mayor, Richard Hatcher, welcomed them. The gathering included the first two African American major-party presidential candidates. One was Jesse Jackson, whose campaigns were several years away, and the other was Shirley Chisholm.

Two months before, Chisholm (D-NY), the first black woman ever elected to Congress, had declared her candidacy for her party's nomination. A self-described "catalyst for change," Chisholm was a committed liberal with solid bona fides in feminist and civil rights circles. In *The Good Fight*, the second of her two memoirs, she wrote, "I ran because someone had to do it first. In this country everybody is supposed to be able to run for president, but that's never been really true. I ran because most people think the country is not ready for a black candidate, not ready for a woman candidate."

Her platform included calls for a minimum annual income of sixty-five hundred dollars for a family of four, the complete withdrawal of American influence in Vietnam, and the denial of all military appropriations "until priorities are reversed." With a slim budget of approximately three hundred thousand dollars, Chisholm campaigned in eleven state primaries over six months, all the way to the July convention in Miami Beach. She received 151.5 first-ballot votes. Chisholm, who remained in Congress until 1982, had intended to establish a helpful precedent for future Americans with similar ambitions. "The next time a woman runs, or a black, a Jew or anyone from a group that the country is 'not ready' to elect to its highest office, I believe he or she will be taken seriously from the start," she wrote. "The door is not open yet, but it is ajar."

By 1976, the number of black elected officials had risen above forty-three hundred. President Jimmy Carter's administration, reflecting his debt to the black voters who helped him win, included more dark faces in visible roles than perhaps ever before. Patricia Roberts Harris (HUD secretary), Clifford Alexander Jr. (secretary of the Army), and Andrew Young (UN ambassador) were among his high-profile appointments, along with Eleanor Holmes Norton (EEOC). Reflecting on blacks' newfound visibility in leadership roles, in 1977 Young told an audience, "We were protest and now we are *it*."

He wasn't just talking about at the federal level. At that

time, Atlanta (Maynard Jackson), Los Angeles (Tom Bradley), and Detroit (Coleman Young) had joined the list of big cities with black mayors, and Bradley had gained precious national exposure as cochair of the Democratic National Convention. These dramatic advances benefited from ambitious and increasingly sophisticated voter registration campaigns. In the South, the number of black voters had doubled since the Voting Rights Act of 1965 was passed. Harold Washington's stunning 1982 victory in Chicago was greatly enabled by a stirring registration campaign that repeatedly roused voters to "Come Alive October 5."

None of these developments escaped the astute attention of Jesse Jackson, who sensed an opportunity of historic proportions. On January 16, 1984, in Philadelphia, Pennsylvania, he announced his candidacy for the Democratic presidential nomination. He told his listeners that instead of resting on their laurels, blacks should join groups with similar interests in a rainbow coalition designed to expand the nation's corridors of power.

"You must never forget that about the time we began to take over the cities, Nixon shifted the power to the suburbs," he warned. "Now Reagan has shifted it to the states. So you have mayors who have more and more responsibility and less and less power. We got more and more votes and fewer and fewer services. We cannot stop. We got to rise on higher."

Written off by many pundits from the start, Jackson's campaign successes startled much of the mainstream media, although few African Americans seemed surprised.

They were behind his third-place finish, during which he became the first African American to win a major-party primary (he won five primaries and caucuses in all). He captured 3,282,431 primary votes, 18.2 percent of the total.

It was dress rehearsal for 1988, when Jackson doubled his previous results. He won 6.9 million votes and eleven contests and, at one point, was his party's front-runner. Though Jackson's platform proposals were deemed too liberal for the Democrats' centrist aims, his campaign provided a tantalizing preview of a committed, multiracial alliance in action.

At the beginning of his first run, Jackson had pointed out the difficulties black candidates faced when running for statewide office. They always collided with a brick wall of resistance when forced to range beyond the black constituencies that formed their base. Undoubtedly Los Angeles mayor Tom Bradley was one of the politicians Jackson had in mind. Although he was capable and popular among the multiracial liberals of L.A., Bradley fell down in the rest of the state. He lost elections for governor in 1982 and 1986. His 1982 defeat came despite polls suggesting a significant advantage over his white opponent.

There's an 80 percent chance in the next election that I will tell all my friends I'm voting for Barack Obama but I'll vote for John McCain.

—Liz Lemon (Tina Fey) in the "Fireworks" episode of
30 Rock

The gap between white voters' poll responses and their actual votes has since been termed "the Bradley effect." A similar disparity nearly prevented L. Douglas Wilder from becoming the first black man in American history to be elected governor when he claimed Virginia's top post in 1989.

Still, unlike Bradley or Andrew Young, loser of a 1990 bid for governor of Georgia, Wilder managed what can only be called a crossover success. At about 15 percent black, Virginia has the smallest number of African Americans of any of the southern states. Wilder's victory proved that persuading large numbers of white voters was difficult but not impossible.

Unsurprisingly, Wilder thought his triumph contained many useful lessons for Obama to study and learn from. "I used to say it this way: 'I don't want anyone to vote for me because of my race, but I don't want anyone to vote against me because of my race.' In other words, I don't want race to be either a badge or a barrier. It's not a color-blind society we live in, and I hope we never do live in a color-blind society. I just want the colors to make no difference."

Wilder's subsequent candidacy for president in 1992 may have also been instructive. It lasted only four months and had little success attracting black support. But his unprecedented reign at Virginia's statehouse remains a textbook example of downplaying race and emphasizing common interests.

Until Obama, no one was better positioned to take advantage of the changing tide than Colin Powell. In the fall of 1995, he had just concluded a triumphant promotional tour for his hugely successful memoir, *My American Journey*. Huge, adoring crowds had greeted him across the country, and his popularity seemed to know no limits. In September a Gallup poll measured "significantly higher" favorability ratings for Powell than for any other potential candidate in the 1996 race. "Running as a Republican in a two-way race against Bill Clinton," the poll said, "Powell handily beats the sitting president, 54% to 39%."

In an afterword added to subsequent printings of the book, Powell recalled that for three weeks after the tour, "I received a huge volume of mail encouraging me to run. 'Powell for President' committees sprang up all over. Campaign buttons and bumper stickers appeared. . . . Several Republican Party leaders urged me to enter the race. . . . A delegation of congressional Democrats even asked to meet with me to pursue the idea of my challenging President Clinton for the Democratic nomination."

Powell admitted being "desperately torn." His wife, in contrast, "remained unalterably opposed."

After deep soul-searching, Powell concluded that "the calling was not there. I could not bring to the quest the passion, commitment, and drive I had brought to every day of my thirty-five years in the Army."

Powell's announcement that he would not run was

greeted by widespread disappointment across party lines. Notwithstanding concerns about the Bradley effect, large numbers of whites had supported, even encouraged a black man to run for president of the United States. And he had turned them down.

As it often does, pop culture moved in to satisfy the appetites of a populace demonstrably eager for the kind of leadership that Powell seemed to represent: calm, principled—and black, but not threateningly so.

In 1998 Morgan Freeman soothed a traumatized nation with his dulcet tones as President Tom Beck in *Deep Impact,* a movie about a comet on a collision course with the earth. At the movie's climax, President Beck makes a speech in front of the partially rebuilt U.S. Capitol. "Life will go on. We will prevail," he promises. And he did: *Deep Impact* became an unexpected blockbuster, grossing $350 million. Freeman's performance evidently earned him a promotion. In 2003 he took on the first of two performances as God in the box-office smash *Bruce Almighty.* That same year, Chris Rock's streetwise turn in *Head of State* got lukewarm reviews but the movie still managed to rank as No. 1 its opening weekend, with $14 million in box-office receipts.

But Dennis Haysbert contributed the most satisfying— and Powell-esque—vision of the presidency that could have been. Strong, square-jawed, and ramrod straight, Haysbert's President Palmer was not only ideally qualified for the job but also perfectly equipped to convince voters of his suitability. And his blackness was handled very subtly. Even his being stalked by killers was linked to political conspirators instead of, say, white supremacists, as it was in *The Man*.

Howard Gordon, an executive producer of *24,* told the *Los Angeles Times* that he and his colleagues downplayed Palmer's race because "it was a cooler thing to do than not to do. Race was subverted in many of the ways that Obama subverts race. It does make it more interesting from a narrative point of view." And, to be sure, from an electoral one as well.

Haysbert also saw the connection. Just as Powell's real-life unprecedented popularity among voters of all races (at least before his UN debacle) helped prepare them for an Obama, so, too, did the fictional and highly popular David Palmer. At least that's how Haysbert views it, and he definitely has a point.

"What my role did and the way I was able to play it, plus the way the writers wrote it, opened the eyes of the American people, from the poorest to the richest, of every color and creed, that a black president was viable and could happen."

In short, David Palmer was a long way from Rufus Jones.

Writing in *Newsweek,* Joshua Alston worried that in the sterling Haysbert and the stalwart Geena Davis (in the short-lived *Commander-in-Chief,* about a woman president), "Hollywood is building unreasonable expectations for our real-life candidates."

No danger. We can rely on real life—and our own government—to supply some balance. That is, at least where
black elected officials are concerned. Statistics suggest that
they have been disproportionately targeted by law enforce-
ment agencies.

Black elected officials were targeted for investigation
of corruption in 14 percent of the 465 corruption cases
probed between 1983 and 1988—"a period in which
blacks were just 3 percent of all officeholders," according to the *Washington Post*. *GQ* magazine reached a similar conclusion: because nearly half of the Congressional
Black Caucus were subjects of investigations or indict-
ments between 1981 and 1993, "for the numbers to be
equal for the white representatives, 204 of the 409 whites
. . . would have been subjected to the same scrutiny during that time, . . . yet, according to Justice Dept. figures,
only 15 actually were."

It's certainly possible that black lawmakers are significantly more corrupt than their nonblack counterparts, but
it's statistically improbable at best. Still wondering why conspiracy theories are so popular with some African Americans? The rate at which the feds go after black politicians
recalls the fear of black power that so aroused white politicians eager to reconcile North and South that they brought
Reconstruction to a crashing halt. They called it "Negro
domination" back then.

Remnants of that fear were wittily exposed by sharp

satirists like Jon Stewart, who brought it up during an interview with Obama on the eve of the Pennsylvania Democratic primary. He asked the candidate, "If you are fortunate enough to get the Democratic nomination, fortunate enough to become president of the United States, will you pull a bait-and-switch, sir, and enslave the white race? Is that your plan?"

It's the fear savagely ridiculed in Richard Pryor's classic 1977 sketch about the first black president (easily accessible on YouTube). During a press conference, a buttoned-down commander in chief (Pryor) gradually loosens up and begins to reveal his "real" agenda. It includes installing Black Panther Huey Newton as the director of the FBI, signing more black quarterbacks to NFL contracts, and playing jazz on NASA missions. "No more will they have the same kinds of music—Beethoven, Brahms, and Tchaikovsky," he declares. "From now on we're gonna have Miles Davis and Charlie Parker."

My own favorite comedic take on the phenomenon is ably displayed in *Undercover Brother,* a 2002 over-the-top race comedy that has attracted a cult following. Chris Kattan plays Mr. Feather, a villainous henchman in a white-racist conspiracy. As he sees it, racial harmony would spell the death of "white" culture.

He complains to an ally, "You see how we're being corrupted by their hip and now fashion and their cool slang you can't help but use? . . . Little by little we're blending and merging until one day we're all going to be one united people, living and working and dancing together like the news or Ally McBeal or the people who work at Saturn. We gotta stop it before it's too late."

Kattan's bit would be even more sidesplitting if not for polls suggesting that some folks take such scenarios seriously. Polls, for example, like the New York Times–CBS News poll conducted last August, which found that 16 percent of white voters feared an Obama administration would "favor blacks over whites." They did realize that *The Daily Show* is a comedy, right?

Admittedly, 16 percent is a small percentage, but as Charles Blow noted in the *New York Times,* "If the percentage of white voters who cannot bring themselves to vote for a black candidate were only 15 percent, that would be more than all black voters combined."

But such a setback, however disheartening, would have been merely temporary. The tentative journey begun by Robert Smalls and his colleagues amid the ash and rubble of the Reconstruction had become a steady procession.

At the end of 2007, there were forty-seven black mayors of cities with populations above fifty thousand, including Philadelphia, Detroit, Baltimore, and Washington, D.C. At the end of 2007, there were forty-five blacks holding statewide offices, including Obama in Illinois and Deval Patrick, governor of Massachusetts.

Similarly, the steady push begun by Shirley Chisholm had also gained momentum. It, too, would become an irresistible force—if not in 2008, then in the not-so-distant future. The door she pressed against with such determination was now more than ajar; it was wide open. Sooner or later, someone was bound to walk through.

CHAPTER 4 Leading Men

HE WAS TALL and dark, with a bright smile and a so-norous voice. Highly educated, he had plans to return to Africa and do great things for his people. With his new white wife at his side, he'd apply his learning to saving lives and helping the continent thrive. But his intended's father had serious reservations about the planned marriage. One of his concerns, he implied, involved any children that might result from the union. Sure, it was the sixties and times were changing, but they still had a ways to go. The black intellectual assured his future father-in-law that the bride-to-be had no such worries where offspring were concerned.

"She feels that every single one of our children will be president of the United States," he said. "Your daughter is a bit optimistic. I'd settle for secretary of state."

Even in a movie as steeped in liberal pieties as *Guess Who's Coming to Dinner,* the idea of a child with African ancestry growing up to mount a serious campaign for president, let alone get elected, sounded wildly optimistic. But hey, it was late 1967. Six months earlier, in the cloistered chambers of the Supreme Court, the justices had struck down antimiscegenation laws in *Loving v. Virginia.* What's more, a black man, Sidney Poitier, was king of the box office. In addition to *Guess Who's Coming to Dinner,* he had starred in two more of the year's biggest movies, *In the Heat of the Night* and *To Sir, with Love.* Who could be sure any longer what was possible and what was not?

Matt Drayton, the reluctant father played by Spencer Tracy in *Guess Who's Coming to Dinner,* believed he had a clear idea of society's limitations. "They don't have a dog's chance," he said when discussing with a friend his daughter's romance. "Not in this country. Not in the whole stinking world."

"They *are* this country," his friend replied. "They'll change this stinking world."

After much soul-searching, Drayton gave his approval. His thinking process appeared to differ little from that of Barack Obama's white grandfather, who had been forced to ponder the same dilemma. "Whether he realized it or not," Obama wrote in his memoir, "the sight of his daughter with a black man offered at some deep unexplored level a window into his own heart."

Because his book unfolds in the same era that *Guess Who's Coming to Dinner* portrays, it's not especially remarkable that some scenes closely mirror each other. For example, in the movie, Poitier's character quickly wins over the startled parents with his intelligence, composure, and charisma. When Obama tries to imagine his grandparents' reaction to meeting Barack Sr. for the first time, his vision is not much different: "When the evening is over, they'll both remark on how intelligent the young man seems, so dignified, with the measured gestures, the graceful draping of one leg over another—and how about that accent?"

Still, the connection between Obama and Poitier is stronger and more complicated than that. In his biography, *Obama: From Promise to Power,* David Mendell quotes a campaign manager who had been watching a focus group's reaction to Obama. It was 2003, and Obama was locked in a senate race with two well-funded and well-connected opponents. The moderator was discussing the candidates with a group of "liberal, North Shore women voters, thirty-five to fifty-five and fifty-five plus." When he asked the ladies who each candidate reminded them of, one answered that the first candidate brought Dan Quayle to mind. The second, a woman said, reminded her of someone "embalmed."

"And she looked at Barack," the manager recalled, "and the lady said, 'Sidney Poitier.' At that moment, I was like, 'Shit, this is real!'"

I chuckled when I read that. I wanted to mock the woman's response. So if a candidate is black, handsome, and suave, he has to remind her of Poitier? But I reconsidered when Robert Johnson, the black media billionaire who found new and creative ways to embarrass himself while campaigning for Hillary Clinton, also linked Obama to Sidney Poitier. He came not to praise Obama but to ridicule him. The candidate's behavior, he said, didn't fit "a guy that says I want to be a reasonable, likable Sidney Poitier *Guess Who's Coming to Dinner*. And I'm thinking to myself, this ain't a movie, Sidney."

Johnson's critiques of Obama weren't taken seriously—and there's no reason they should have been—but I do think his mention of Poitier helps to establish the connection. The more I thought about it, the more it made sense. Just as Michael Jackson, Michael Jordan, and other black pop-culture icons helped reshape society and enable Obama's breakthrough, so, too, did Poitier. By the seventies, Poitier's critics had begun to confuse the characters he played with the man himself. Like Jimi Hendrix, he ran into unfriendly observers who found his style out-of-date and insufficiently black.

In the second of his two memoirs, *The Measure of a Man,*
Poitier took aim at some of the criticism he had faced:
"So the question being raised was, What's the message here? That black people will be accepted by white
society only when they're twice as 'white' as the most
accomplished Ivy League medical graduate? That blacks
must pretend to be something they aren't? Or simply
that black society does—of course—contain individuals of refinement, education, and accomplishment, and
that white society—of course—should wake up to that
reality?"

It now seems apparent that Poitier's roles made possible much of the black theatrical and cinematic success
that followed.

In 2002, when Denzel Washington became the first
African American man since Poitier to win an Academy
Award for best actor, he paid tribute to the pioneer who had
led the way.

"Forty years I've been chasin' Sidney," Washington said,
looking up to the balcony where Poitier sat holding an hon-
orary Oscar he'd received earlier in the evening. "They finally give it to me and what'd they do? They give it to him
the same night. I'll always be chasing you, Sidney. I'll always
be following in your footsteps. There's nothing I would
rather do, sir. Nothing I would rather do." The auditorium
erupted in applause as the two men raised their trophies in
mutual salute. The simple, touching gesture expressed an

unassailable truth. No Poitier, no Washington. No Poitier, no Jamie Foxx, no Forest Whitaker. And, quite possibly, no Barack Obama.

In *Guess Who's Coming to Dinner,* we meet Dr. John Wade Prentice (Poitier) at the San Francisco airport. Arm in arm with Joanna, his white fiancée, he heads to her parents' home to meet them for the first time. Their home is rich and palatial with a dazzling view of the great outdoors. Matt Drayton, a newspaper publisher, has a study lined with books and photos. Dr. Prentice takes a look around while placing a phone call. Clearly he can see that the room has a certain baronial splendor.

Obama recalls a similar journey in his memoir. One weekend while living in New York after college, he accompanied his white girlfriend to her family's country home. "It was autumn, beautiful, with woods all around us," he writes. "The library was filled with old books and pictures of the grandfather with famous people he had known— presidents, diplomats, industrialists. There was tremendous gravity to the room."

Dr. Prentice absorbs the wealth and history of his surroundings and decides to gamble his heart on the unlikely chance that Joanna's parents will be won over by his talent and warmth, his good looks and charm. Obama made quite a different decision.

"I realized that our two worlds, my friend's and mine, were as distant from each other as Kenya is from Germany.

And I knew that if we stayed together I'd eventually live in hers." Soon after, the relationship ended.

Obama was young, inexperienced. Prentice is thirty-seven, a widower who has witnessed the best and worst that life has to offer. In many ways, he can be seen as a slightly older version of Gordon Ralfe, the character Poitier had played two years before in *A Patch of Blue*.

In that film, set in New York City, Poitier plays a white-collar professional of undetermined occupation, although from the looks of his workplace he could be a journalist of some sort. He forms an unlikely friendship with a blind white girl—a relationship fairly humming with sexual current.

He meets Selina when she's sitting under a tree in a park. In the first of two extraordinary scenes, he comes upon the distraught girl, inserts his hand into her blouse, and pulls a caterpillar from the small of her back. It's broad daylight, 1965, and a black man has his hand in a white woman's blouse. But the blind girl isn't alarmed. In fact, she's comforted. To her, Gordon radiates strength and calm.

"Your voice sounds very tall," she tells him. "You sound like the radio. Different. Kind of sure."

That description is not much different from Joanna's description of Dr. Prentice in *Guess Who*. "He's so calm and sure of everything," she tells her mother. "He doesn't have any tensions in him."

By 1967, Poitier's smooth exterior had become a trademark. Notwithstanding criticisms that his characters were sexually repressed, his apparent serenity radiates its own kind of seduction. Neither his on-screen lovers nor his off-screen admirers failed to notice that an absence of tension often means the presence of cool. While effortlessly attractive to women, his subtle approach reassured the white men in the audience.

Obama had discovered the rewards of subtlety while still in high school. That's when he noticed "people were satisfied so long as you were courteous and smiled and made no sudden moves. They were more than satisfied; they were relieved—such a pleasant surprise to find a well-mannered young black man who didn't seem angry all the time."

Selina's tragic, impoverished background moves and inspires Gordon Ralfe. He teaches the illiterate girl about Braille, takes her shopping, and shows her how to use a telephone. Quite naturally, Selina falls in love. Being forthright, she tells him.

I love you so much.

Don't be silly, silly.

I do love you.

You hardly know me.

A Patch of Blue is distinctive because it features not one black professional man but two. The second is Gordon's brother Mark. Played by Ivan Dixon, Mark is a hardworking doctor. Like his brother, he is bright, clean, articulate. But he doesn't take kindly to Selina's occasional presence in the apartment the two men share. When Gordon indicates his plans to help her, Mark objects strongly. "The most you're likely to get out of this is a kick in the pants," he warns.

It's not hard to agree with Mark. As Gordon becomes increasingly open in his dealings with Selina, you can almost imagine the forces of whiteness gathering to crush him. But they never arrive. Alone in the apartment, Selina and Gordon kiss passionately before he manages to pull away. Unlike Dr. Prentice, and more like the young Obama, Gordon foresees unhappiness ahead should the two stay together.

"I believe there are reasons why it won't work out," he tells her. However, little supporting evidence appears in the movie. Most whites look on indifferently as Gordon playfully zooms down the grocery aisles with Selina giggling on his cart. They pay no mind at all when he escorts her in and out of his well-appointed apartment building. And, in the second extraordinary scene, they watch with minimal interest when Selina's mother and grandfather confront Gordon in the park. He actually smacks her mother's hand and gathers Selina, who has fallen, in his embrace.

"Did you see that? He struck me," Selina's mom tells the crowd of white onlookers. "He struck me! Isn't anybody going to do nothin'?"

No one does a thing.

Director Guy Green, who adapted the screenplay from a novel by Elizabeth Kata, said that in the book the crowd comes up and chases Gordon away. He said that in the course of completing the first draft of the script, he was "overtaken by events."

"Things became liberalized," he said, leading him to "rewrite the third act." He made the changes in part because "Sidney liked his image as a respectable gentleman."

Poitier came to view respect as a pivotal, even crucial aspect of the characters he inhabited on-screen. Dignity and discipline were uppermost, even if it meant sacrificing a little credibility in scenes such as the one described above. He wrote in *The Measure of a Man,* "When I realized that I could be a better than utilitarian actor, I realized that I had the responsibility, not as a black man, but as an artist, to exercise tremendous discipline. I knew the public would take my measure, and that was constantly in my calculations."

Poitier also likely knew that the public measure of black performers—theatrical, musical, or political—who preceded him was seldom if ever fair. Perhaps he spoke so articulately because in 1825, when Ira Aldridge became the first black actor to perform the role of Othello in London, the London *Times* declared, "Owing to the shape of his lips it is utterly impossible for him to pronounce English." Perhaps he was so restrained in his on-screen romances with white actresses because he knew audiences would frown on any sign of aggression. He doubtless knew about the resistance Paul Robeson met when, 105 years after Aldridge, he took on *Othello* in London. When asked about his love scenes with the white actress Peggy Ashcroft, Robeson told a New Jersey paper, "People objecting to my kissing Miss Ashcroft must realize that she is supposed to be my wife. . . . They certainly wouldn't stand in America for the kissing and for the scene in which I use Miss Ashcroft roughly. I wouldn't care to play those scenes in some parts of the United States. The audience would get rough; in fact, might become dangerous."

Robeson understood that he and Desdemona would hardly be alone on an American stage. They would have to share it with a past so full of lies and harmful myths that his rich baritone, no matter how beautifully rendered, would have been powerless against it. Those myths were compiled and perpetuated by Thomas Jefferson, who popularized the idea that black men were not only "more ardent" than whites but preferred white women. They were waved before white men like a red flag by black heavyweight champ Jack Johnson, who seemed determined to make a prophet of Jefferson. They were made official code by the miscegenation laws of the South. Of white America's many peculiar racial neuroses, those involving sex between white women and black men were most toxic of all.

Fear of exactly that kind of coupling often led to murder and unspeakable mutilations. "It is certain that lynching mobs have not only refused to give the Negro a chance to defend himself, but have killed their victim with a full knowledge that the relationship of the alleged assailant with the woman who accused him, was voluntary and clandestine," wrote the antilynching crusader Ida B. Wells. In the white imagination, such liaisons could never result from mutual consent, hence the popular use of rape charges to, in the words of DuBois, "arouse the worst passions of the countryside."

Poitier bore the history and the prospect of those passions on his shoulders, and he carried them with, yes, dignity, and admirable flair. His longtime friend Harry Belafonte had no patience with such heavy loads. He had shared one of American cinema's first interracial kisses (with Joan Fontaine in *Island in the Sun*) in 1957. Although the film had been banned in the South and at least one theater was firebombed, Belafonte survived the controversy and was poised to become a top movie star. But he rejected many of the roles offered to him, including parts Poitier ultimately accepted in *Lilies of the Field* and *To Sir, with Love*. He told the *Washington Post* he turned them down because they were " 'neutered,' with little sexuality or humanity."

Belafonte ultimately discovered in dramatic fashion that *any* contact between a black man and a white woman could stir up white anger. His brief contact with white singer Petula Clark during an NBC special on April 2, 1967, provoked a fierce and hostile reaction. Producer-director Steve Binder, who worked on the show, later told an interviewer that executives from sponsor Plymouth-Chrysler initially opposed Belafonte's being on the show, because he was black. Once that was settled, Clark and Belafonte shot three takes of a duet. On the fourth take, Clark reached out and touched Belafonte's forearm.

Plymouth executives on the set immediately stormed out. "I thought a herd of elephants had just left the client's booth," Binder said. "You'd have thought they fornicated on the show. I went down to the editing room with Petula's husband and we made the editor erase the first three takes so that the only take we had was the last take, with them touching."

Binder called the furor that erupted "an international incident." He said there were big stories in *Time, Newsweek,* and elsewhere. "I was so naive," said Binder. "I couldn't believe in 1967 this was still going on, but it was the first time a black and a white had touched in prime-time television."

A similar gesture attracts a glare of concern in *Love Field,* a 1992 film starring Dennis Haysbert and Michelle Pfeiffer. The two have just witnessed Lee Harvey Oswald's murder on live television when Haysbert, playing Paul Cater, consoles Pfeiffer by touching her arm. Pfeiffer plays Lurene Hallett, a dissatisfied Texas housewife grieving the death of President Kennedy. A series of dramatic misunderstandings have placed Paul and Lurene on the lam in the Deep South, with Paul's young daughter in tow.

The film's 1963 setting places it just a few years earlier than *Guess Who's Coming to Dinner*. But where Joanna Drayton's insistent belief in the possibility of racial harmony is cast as evidence of changing times, Lurene's similar optimism is exposed as naive and uninformed. When Lurene informs a poor black mechanic that President Kennedy has "done a lot" for his people, the mechanic eyes her quizzically. "Take a look around, ma'am," he says. "Look like he done much around here?"

When their car stalls in a lonely southern town, Lurene tells Paul that strangers will come to assist them because "this country's full of good, trusting people." Not much later, a trio of white locals drives up and beats Paul to a bloody pulp. So much for good and trusting.

Eventually, Lurene and Paul find common ground and enjoy a sexual tryst in a barn. The scene is brief, soft-focus, and hazily lit. If *Love Field* had been filmed in 1963, Poitier most likely would have played Paul. Haysbert does well in his stead. Also tall, dark, and handsome, Haysbert's Paul is long-suffering and patient. Because it was filmed in 1992, Paul gets to occasionally vent his frustration at Lurene as well as act upon his sexual attraction to her. Where Poitier and his white love interests offered hope of reconciliation through chaste romantic love, Paul promises fulfillment of a much earthier variety.

Though *Love Field* performed quietly at the box office, it remains noteworthy not only because it was the first leading role for Haysbert, but because Denzel Washington was initially slated to play Paul but backed out. Washington allegedly told *Newsweek* reporter Allison Samuels that he dropped out because he objected to the racial language in the script. "It was nigger this and nigger that," Samuels quotes him as saying. "I wasn't going to be but so many niggers in a film."

Some observers speculated that Washington had gotten cold feet about playing Pfeiffer's lover. He famously declined to play a love scene with Julia Roberts in *The Pelican Brief,* filmed a year after *Love Field.* Washington told Samuels that his avoidance of interracial couplings stemmed from negative audience reaction to a romantic scene with white actress Mimi Rogers in *The Mighty Quinn.* From then on he resolved to consider the feelings of African American women. "Black women are not often seen as objects of desire on film," he said. "They have always been my core audience."

The only black man ever chosen *People* magazine's "sexiest man alive," Washington clearly has many, many white female admirers as well. In fact, his being chosen in 1996 represents a sort of tipping point, especially when considered alongside other cultural developments that we've observed thus far.

In a retrospective article, *People* quoted African American movie producer Debra Martin Chase, who recalled that Washington's selection "solidified his position as a sex symbol, not just an African-American sex symbol. It's a sign of the times that we can say you don't have to look like Brad Pitt to be the sexiest man. It expands the idea of what's beautiful."

Once mainstream audiences demonstrated emphatically (through box-office and media coverage) that they were willing to accept black men as fully sexualized leading men, they became even more inclined to accept them as *leaders* of men.

Washington's donation of twenty-three hundred dollars to Obama's campaign isn't the only factor connecting the two men. (Poitier was also a contributor.) The movie star's sex-symbol status and the politician's glamorous aura lend the pair powerful media presences that help offset negative depictions of African American men. It's hard to think of any image that has received more coverage in the past two years than Obama's intelligent, confident, smiling face.

Tyra Banks: In a movie where they are doing the autobiography of Senator Barack Obama, who would play you?

Obama: Initially, Denzel would be the choice, but somebody pointed out that with my ears it might have to be Will. Will Smith.

On the *Oprah Winfrey Show,* Julia Roberts talked about being on location with Washington and finding "200 women just screaming" outside his trailer. "It was like working with the Beatles," she said.

Similar analogies were often drawn in descriptions

of Obama's campaign appearances before large crowds. Writing in the *Nation,* JoAnn Wypijewski reported seeing "legions of little girls jumping out of their panties" during a 2006 Obama stop in Virginia. "He glided across the stage like a crooner, one slender hand gracing the microphone, the other extending long fingers to trace the imagined horizon of his hopes and dreams," she wrote. "He was Frank Sinatra, so cool he's hot, a centrifugal force commanding attention so ruthlessly that it appeared effortless, reducing everyone around him to a sidekick, and the girls in the front rows to jelly."

Watching him move a crowd in England, a British journalist was just as effusive. "Imagine the cool cred of a Steve McQueen, the black charisma of a Denzel Washington, the lean athleticism of a young Mick Jagger, and you have a politician made partly out of rock star and partly out of movie idol," he enthused. "He's not just a terrific orator, he has sex appeal too."

Obama's youthful vigor and attractiveness—uncommon in national political contests—prompted an outpouring of Internet parodies, tributes, and mashups. Some are subtle, while others get right to the point. Such as the famous Obama Girl video, for example, in which a buxom white brunette lip-synchs that the candidate of her dreams is "smart," "black," "sexy," and "fine." That such "tributes" have done little to stir up age-old psychosexual anxieties is both a wonder and a testament to changing times.

McCain's team, frustrated by Obama's thunderous

responses from huge crowds, began to lampoon their opponent in ads like "Fan Club," in which Obama was contemptuously dismissed as a "rock star." Women were shown comparing him to Bono and praising his "very soft eyes."

"We know that he doesn't have much experience," a voice intoned, "and that he isn't ready to lead. But that doesn't mean he isn't dreamy."

The McCain spot merely echoed press pieces that tried to suggest that Obama was little more than an empty suit— an empty, elegant, well-tailored suit. Or even a bathing suit: to Obama's apparent chagrin, a photo of him romping in the surf appeared in a magazine in January 2007 alongside shots of Hugh Jackman, Penelope Cruz, and other Hollywood celebrities. The feature was headlined "Beach Babes."

As shallow as such items were, they probably won Obama a few votes. But they frustrated him anyway. "I know that one of the running threads, or one of the narratives that's established itself among the mainstream media is this notion 'Well, you know, Obama has pretty good style, he can deliver a pretty good speech, but he seems to prioritize rhetoric over substance,'" he complained to the press. "The problem is that that's not what you guys have been reporting on. You've been reporting how I look in a swimsuit."

In truth, the "Fan Club" ad was both typical attack-dog politics and evidence of the extraordinarily concentrated gaze that Obama labored under each day of the campaign. It was not the same as that faced by John McCain.

In his memoir, Sidney Poitier recalls having to undergo an audition of sorts for Katharine Hepburn, with whom he was to costar in *Guess Who's Coming to Dinner*. He endured her scrutiny with good cheer despite already having made more than thirty films and winning an Oscar.

"I could tell that I was being sized up every time I spoke, every response I made," he wrote. "I could imagine a plus and a minus column, notations in her mind."

Poitier went along with the "tests" because he knew Hepburn and Tracy were contemplating a maiden voyage. "They were going to enter into an intense creative partnership with a black man," he wrote, "a partnership in which they would take on one of the primal taboos of our culture, interracial marriage."

"Intense creative partnership with a black man" strikes me as an apt metaphor for an electorate willing to vote a candidate like Obama into the nation's highest office. For the partnership to work, Obama would have to step more carefully than any presidential candidate before him. Like Poitier, Obama occasionally frustrated his supporters by appearing too tolerant, too willing to suffer the slings and arrows of outrage aimed at him and, as often, at his wife. One misguided suggestion from Arianna Huffington called for Obama to channel Martin Luther King Jr.'s prophetic anger, conveniently forgetting that black rage, even when righteous and fully articulated, can lead to quite different and fatal consequences. As King himself put it, "In the life of Negro civil rights leaders, the whine of the bullet from ambush, the roar of the bomb have all too often broken the night's silence."

Nor have many white observers shown the ability to distinguish among the varieties of "prophetic" anger that contribute to black tradition. From that confusion arose media questions and comments linking Obama's criticisms of American policy to Jeremiah Wright's fiery sermons while failing to note any connection to King's pointed critiques. It was King, after all, who argued that Americans "have committed more war crimes almost than any nation in the world."

Therefore Obama's decision to emphasize calm over passion during his debates with McCain was a prudent choice. By the third debate, McCain's fury at having to share the stage with an impudent upstart—an upstart with an expanding lead in the polls—was evident in every twitch and eye-rolling grimace. Watching McCain choke and sputter, I recalled Ralph Ellison's timeless observation that "the maintenance of dignity is never a simple matter, even for those of highest credentials."

Trying to make good on his promise to go out and "whip his you-know-what," McCain went negative and further wounded his floundering campaign. "For a punch to make a difference, the punch needs to do something to its target," the *New York Times* noted. But McCain's jabs drew no blood nor self-defeating counterpunches, leaving Obama "calm, cool and collected for the most part." Harold Meyerson, writing in the *Washington Post,* judged the outcome in similar terms: "John of the Grimaces met Barack the Unflappable in Hempstead tonight, and the guy with the arctic cool, not surprisingly, prevailed." Obama's goal, he wrote, "was to look resolute, but also to be the world's least angry—or more precisely, anger-able—black man."

Meyerson understood that Obama, compared with McCain, had a much smaller margin of error. If he avoided fighting fire with fire he was seen as being too passive; if he pointed out his opponents' tactics, he was accused of playing the race card and wallowing in politics-as-usual. Never mind that his brown skin made it hard for viewers to trace any of that unflappability to his white grandparents' "straight-backed form of Methodism that valued reason over passion and temperance over both," as he described it in *Dreams from My Father.* The trap he struggled to avoid was made of ignorance and illogic, forming a cage with which Obama was distressingly familiar. He had already written eloquently about the folly of a black man resorting to rage. Should he do so, he warned, "they would have a name for that, too, a name that could cage you just as good. Paranoid. Militant. Violent. Nigger."

The cage of calumny that Obama's enemies tried to

construct around him closely resembled the trap that he described, with perhaps a few variations to suit the post-9/11 era: "Paranoid." "Muslim." "Naive." "Terrorist." Every libelous label seemed carefully designed to suit the uncertainty of our time. When a man's innocuous fist bump with his wife could be described to an audience of millions as a gesture of rebel solidarity, who could be sure any longer what was possible and what was not?

CHAPTER 5 Figures of Speech

THE DEMOCRATIC PARTY ... never had an opening night like this before," the *Washington Times* said of Barbara Jordan's convention keynote speech in 1976, "and never will again."

To say that the *Times,* like the rest of us, failed to foresee Obama's sparkling convention debut nearly three decades in the future doesn't diminish Jordan's accomplishment in the slightest. For many Americans who witnessed her performance, it was a showstopping introduction. For Jordan, it was just the latest in a string of history-making entrances. Four years earlier, she had become the first black woman elected to Congress from the South. On July 12 of our country's bicentennial year, she became the first African American to deliver the keynote address at a major party's national convention. Only twelve years had passed since another black woman, Fannie Lou Hamer, had spoken eloquently before a Democratic convention credentials committee in a historic but unsuccessful bid to be seated as a delegate. Jordan made no mention of Hamer in her speech but wryly noted that in the years since her party's first convention in 1832, "it would have been most unusual for any national political party" to ask someone like her to speak.

Jordan had distinguished herself during the Watergate hearings as a lawmaker with a steady gaze and incisive candor. An attorney and an experienced debater, Jordan had a stern, almost formal style, and she spoke in a clear, resolute, and ringing voice. Apparently having little patience for preening or grandstanding, she spoke on July 12 with the zeal of a prosecutor, so intent upon making her points that she frequently talked right through the audience's applause. But, as Obama would do in his own keynote twenty-eight years later, she focused not on indictment but conciliation.

"I could easily spend this time praising the accomplishments of this party and attacking the Republicans," she began, "but I don't choose to do that. I could list the problems which cause people to feel cynical, angry, frustrated . . . but I don't choose to do that either."

Jordan went on to downplay the conventional divisions

between liberals and conservatives, instead emphasizing the values and desires that all Americans have in common. In her view, the United States could recover from the disaster of Watergate only if its leaders struck a balance between the idea that government must be active in the lives of its citizens and the belief that it should intervene as little as possible. "In this election year we must define the common *good* and begin again to shape a common future," she urged. But that kind of convergence could not take place unless "each of us remembers that we share a common destiny."

Although she was the daughter of a minister, Jordan's oratory owed less to the pulpit than to the debate competitions in which she had won honors as an undergraduate and the law school classrooms where she had honed her skills. In a 1979 interview with the *Washington Post,* she stressed the value of her legal training. "I could no longer orate and let that pass for reasoning," she said. "Because there was not any demand for an orator in Boston University law school. You had to think and read and understand and reason. I had learned at 21 that you couldn't just say a thing is so, because it might not be so, and somebody brighter, smarter, and more thoughtful would come out and tell you it wasn't so. Then if you still thought it was, you had to prove it."

That is the tradition of African American eloquence to which Obama properly belongs. It owes a partial debt to black ministers, at least to the extent that clergymen have often played a pivotal role in black advocacy. But it derives more substantially from activist intellectuals who have mastered both emotional flights of rhetoric and reasoned argument, who have seldom confused volume with clarity or rhyming with logic. The most able black clergymen, preachers such as Martin Luther King Jr. and Vernon Johns, embodied the best of this tradition. Under their capable stewardship, the church often functioned as James Baldwin (a former preacher himself) described it: "the place where protest and condemnation could be most vividly articulated." But their example stands out all the more against a far less sterling group that has long specialized in, to borrow from James Brown, "talking loud and saying nothing."

In contrast, the line of black eloquence leading through Jordan and on to Obama amounts to a Keatsian grand march of intellect. Its common themes, discussed below, are usually composed of the following elements: illumination, in which the speaker outlines the social, political, and economic condition of blacks (or all Americans); advocacy, in which the speaker proposes or outlines a plan to improve those conditions; instruction, which usually emphasizes the responsibility of individual citizens to enable their own uplift; hope, which previews what life will be like after conditions are improved; and conciliation, which describes the widespread peace and harmony that will inevitably result when the other improvements are accomplished.

Because of that legacy, eloquence is well known, even expected, by black audiences. But when a black speaker reveals her gifts before a mainstream audience, the reaction often is one of awe. The *Washington Post* wrote that the 1976 Democratic National Convention "erupted in pandemonium" when Jordan's voice was heard, at the beginning of a film preceding her address, saying, "If there is such a thing as a patriot in this country, then I am one." In addition, "when she delivered her statement as a member of the House Judiciary Committee considering the impeachment of Richard Nixon ('My faith in the Constitution is whole. It is complete. It is total.') . . . many Americans wept."

That description is easily recalled when sifting through liberal media reactions to Obama, who, as Sam Anderson gushed in *New York* magazine, has "delivered more game-changing speeches than most politicians muster in a full career." After Obama's 2004 convention keynote, Anderson writes, "America watched him rip off the rumpled suit of anonymous, mild-mannered state-senatorhood and squeeze into the gaudy cape and tights of our national oratorical superhero—a honey-tongued Frankenfusion of Lincoln, Gandhi, Cicero, Jesus, and all our most cherished national acronyms (MLK, JFK, RFK, FDR)."

The *New Yorker*'s George Packer recalled hearing an Obama "speech that dissolved into pure feeling for days," although he couldn't remember what the candidate had said. Jennifer Rubin, writing in the *New York Observer* in June 2008, considered what McCain could do to overcome the "rhetoric gap." Earlier in the campaign, Hillary Clinton had tried and failed to surmount that same gap. Despite Obama's repeated declarations that the road to change "is never easy," she joked that his listeners came to hear "celestial choirs" and assurances that "the world will be perfect." McCain, for his part, warned that Obama's message was "an eloquent but empty call for change" that was not only unbelievable but deliberately deceitful as well.

More than a century before Obama emerged to astonish his admirers and perplex his opponents, Frederick Douglass experienced a similar rise. By 1845, when he published *Narrative of the Life of Frederick Douglass: An American Slave*, he had won the admiration of black and white audiences alike. Candid, charismatic, and believed to be of biracial parentage, he became the most influential black person in the history of the young nation.

Yet his eloquent speeches and moving condemnations of slavery failed to persuade every listener. Some critics warned that his ringing oratory and impeccable enunciation had to result from some elaborate scam. After all, they contended, hadn't Thomas Jefferson written that no Negro existed who had "uttered a thought above the level of plain narration"?

Such suspicions had dogged Douglass ever since he entered the public arena. As early as 1841 a supporter had offered this cautious advice: "People won't believe that you were ever a slave, Frederick, if you keep on this way." Another colleague contributed similar counsel: "Better have a little of the plantation speech than not; it is not best that you seem to be learned."

Evidence of Jefferson's lingering ghost was provided by none other than Joseph Biden, Obama's eventual partner on the Democratic ticket. Earlier in the primary season, he unwittingly echoed the author of the Declaration of Independence when he marveled at Obama's ability to bathe regularly and string sentences together. To Biden, the candidate seemed to be a character straight out of fiction. "I mean, you got the first mainstream African-American who is articulate and bright and clean and a nice-looking guy," he declared. "I mean, that's a storybook, man."

"Language is also a political instrument, means, and proof of power," James Baldwin observed. "It is the most vivid and crucial key to identity: It reveals the private identity, and connects one with, or divorces one from, the larger, public, or communal identity." When those whom language has been used to oppress begin to use that language to challenge that oppression—and its attendant stereotypes—complications invariably follow. One consequence that Douglass confronted in 1845 and that Obama often ran into during his campaign was the peril of sounding educated. That peril is not always race-based. As Maureen Dowd noted in the *New York Times,* "The people who want English to be the official language of the United States are uncomfortable with their leaders being fluent in it." When filtered through race, however, the danger takes on an added dimension.

The notion that "learning would *spoil* the best nigger in the world," recounted in Douglass's narrative, fueled the harsh Southern codes that made it illegal for slaves to read. Long before Baldwin, the slaveholding class recognized the close relationship between power and eloquence. In antebellum times, blacks whose speech and mannerisms seemed to reflect an unwillingness to acknowledge their degraded status were condemned as "uppity," or unjustifiably arrogant. To consider how tenacious this notion has been, simply recall that Lynn Westmoreland, a Republican congressman from Georgia, used the u-word to describe the Obamas as recently as September 2008. Political commentator David Gergen, a native southerner, suggested that Westmoreland's description was knowingly racist. In his view such language, along with some of McCain's attack ads, constituted "code for, 'He's uppity, he ought to stay in his place.' Everybody gets that who is from a southern background."

Of course, one didn't have to be a southerner to buy into the idea. That much was true even during the slavery era. Writing in his private journal in 1822, nineteen-year-old Ralph Waldo Emerson recorded his belief that "nobody now regards the maxim 'that all men are born equal' as anything more than a convenient hypothesis or an extravagant declaration." Embracing the myth that his nation's captive Africans found comfort and enrichment in their bondage, Emerson concluded, "the same pleasure and confidence which the dog and horse feel when they rely upon the superior intelligence of man is felt by the lower parts of our species." He offered as evidence his own—incredible—firsthand experience: "I saw ten, twenty, a hundred large-lipped, lowbrowed black men in the streets who, except in the mere matter of language, did not exceed the sagacity of the elephant."

By 1850, Emerson had matured enough to see the folly and injustice of slavery. The enactment of the "filthy" Fugitive Slave Law, he wrote, "was made in the 19th century, by people who could read and write. I will not obey it, by God." For Emerson, what had once been "mere language" had been transformed into a weapon as weighty and damaging as the chains used to drag escaped slaves from New England back to Virginia. Such scenarios must have been what Baldwin had in mind when he wrote, "A language comes into existence by means of brutal necessity, and the rules of the language are dictated by what the language must convey."

In the oratorical tradition to which Obama belongs, black language is often prompted by brutal necessity—or, more precisely, as a response to brutality. Speech, as the actor-rapper Mos Def describes it, becomes a hammer. Not a bludgeon, mind you (except when circumstances demand it), but an instrument of power and leverage—a carpenter's tool useful in constructing arguments that can withstand the buffeting forces of ignorance, suspicion, and ridicule.

It is a tradition of speaking truth to power, as when James T. Rapier, a black Republican from Alabama, took the House floor to argue for passage of the Civil Rights Act of 1875: "The anomalous and, I may add, the supremely ridiculous position of the Negro at this time, in this country, compels me to say something." Although, he added, "the valor of the colored soldier . . . ought to be far more persuasive than any poor language I can command."

It is a tradition of serving as the nation's conscience, of baring truths with unrestrained candor, as John Lewis did at the March on Washington in 1963. He cautioned his listeners against regarding their brief multiracial moment in the sun as evidence of a lasting victory. "This nation is still a place of cheap political leaders who build their careers on immoral compromise and ally themselves with open forms of political, economic, and social exploitation," he warned.

Obama, too, has issued painful, timely reminders. His March 18, 2008, Philadelphia address (aka the "race" speech) in response to the controversy stemming from Rev. Jeremiah Wright's remarks, for example, pulled no punches. Instead of merely assuaging white fears, he outlined a stark future made desolate by shallow jingoism and bait-and-switch political maneuverings. "We have a choice in this country," he argued. "We can tackle race only as spectacle . . . or in the wake of tragedy . . . or as fodder for the nightly news. . . . But if we do, I can tell you that in the next election, we'll be talking about some other distraction. And then another one. And then another one. And nothing will change."

It is a tradition of using our Republic's most beloved words and sacred texts to expose its flawed morality.

Douglass set the standard in an address called "What to the Slave Is the Fourth of July?" It was 1852, not long after Emerson came to his senses. Douglass declared, "I will, in the name of humanity which is outraged, in the name of liberty which is fettered, in the name of the Constitution and the Bible which are disregarded and trampled upon, dare to call in question and to denounce, with all the emphasis I can command, everything that serves to perpetuate slavery—the great sin and shame of America!"

Few American critics have demonstrated such intimate familiarity with their country's secular scriptures as the black orator-activists across the centuries who have challenged us to live up to the meaning of our nation's creed. Marcus Garvey, seventy years and a philosophy apart from the integrationist Douglass, referred just as pointedly to the Founders' lofty principles in his own fervent critique, one that Obama especially might appreciate: "What do I mean by constitutional rights in America? If the black man is to reach the height of his ambition in this country—if the black man is to get all of his constitutional rights in America—then the black man should have the same chance in the nation as any other man to become president of the nation, or a street cleaner in New York."

Fannie Lou Hamer's appearance at the 1964 Democratic convention proved that the denial of constitutional rights remained as troublesome in her day as it was in Garvey's time. Her testimony included graphic descriptions of her torture at the hands of racist southern police. After reciting the bloodcurdling details, Hamer reminded the committee why she was there in the first place. "All of this is on account of we want to register," she said, "to become first-class citizens. And if the Freedom Democratic Party is not seated now, I question America. Is this America, the land of the free and the home of the brave, where we have to sleep with our telephones off of the hooks because our lives be threatened daily, because we want to live as decent human beings, in America?"

Barbara Jordan "was never without a copy of the Constitution in her purse," according to the *New York Times*. It seems fitting, then, that she began her opening statement at the televised Watergate hearings—and held the nation spellbound—with an improvised meditation on that document's Preamble. " 'We the people,' " she said. "It is a very eloquent beginning. But when the Constitution of the United States was completed on the 17th of September in 1787, I was not included in that 'We the people.' I felt for many years that somehow George Washington and Alexander Hamilton just left me out by mistake. But through the process of amendment, interpretation, and court decision, I have finally been included in 'We the people.' "

Consciously or not, Jordan offered a persuasive follow-up to Douglass's Glasgow Address, delivered in 1860. The

Constitution, he argued, said "'we the people;' not we the white people, not even we the citizens, not we the privileged class, not we the high, not we the low, but we the people; not we the horses, sheep, and swine, and wheel-barrows, but we the people, we the human inhabitants; and, if Negroes are people, they are included in the benefits for which the Constitution of America was ordained and established."

Obama began his "race" speech with those same three all-important words. He reminded his listeners that the sacred document beginning with "We the people" was "stained by this nation's original sin of slavery." He went on to acknowledge the Americans of all racial backgrounds who fought and sacrificed because "words on a parchment would not be enough to deliver slaves from bondage, or provide men and women of every color and creed their full rights and obligations as citizens of the United States."

Obama's talk of validation and fulfillment echoed the sentiments of Martin Luther King Jr., whose oratory Obama's resembles in tone and intellectual flavor more than in any other aspects. "In the absence of Martin Luther King," Jesse Jackson Jr. has noted, "the void was filled by Stokely Carmichael, James Bevel and Jesse Jackson. With all respect to my father, 40 years later, this is the first time we have gotten back to a very thoughtful and careful approach to language."

Like the multilingual Vernon Johns or his mentor Benjamin Mays, King frequently gave addresses that were deeply allusive, and not just to biblical passages. He was fond of invoking such timeless thinkers as the eloquent but racist Thomas Carlyle ("No lie can live forever"); Langston Hughes, beloved poet laureate of black America ("I say it plain, / America never was America to me"); and the poet-journalist William Cullen Bryant ("Truth, crushed to earth, will rise again"). As did King—and unlike the pastor-spokesmen who have attempted to follow in King's wake—Obama leaves the listener thinking, "Here is not a man who simply emotes; here is a man who reads." The best addresses of King and Obama exemplify an intellectual form of sermonizing that not only testifies but also confronts, honors, and respectfully questions the traditions (American and African American) to which the men belong. Obama's speechmaking skills recall the qualities Baldwin identified as the keys to King's power as an orator: "his intimate knowledge of the people he is addressing, be they black or white, and the forthrightness with which he speaks of those things which hurt or baffle them." In his last speech, King characterized the battles to which Obama would someday pay tribute as efforts to make the United States "be true to what you said on paper."

Frederick Douglass was so confident of an African American consensus that he could challenge the nation's celebration of the Fourth of July on behalf of all his black countrymen. Accordingly, he asked, "What have I, or *those I represent* [italics added], to do with your national independence?" Conditions were fairly cut-and-dried for blacks in 1852. As Douglass's contemporary Martin Delany, a free black, had bluntly put it, "the bondsman is disfranchised, and for the most part so are we."

In subsequent years, and especially after the Civil War, economic and social diversity began to complicate the notion of "representativeness": it became increasingly difficult, if not impossible, for one individual to presume to speak for all black Americans. So it was for Booker T. Washington, whose accommodationism encountered stiff dissent soon after white power brokers anointed him Douglass's heir. W. E. B. DuBois, his fiercest and most formidable opponent, had no trouble getting to the root of the problem. Everyone in the black community stood to lose irreparably, he said, "a loss of that peculiarly valuable education which a group receives when by search and criticism it finds and commissions its own leaders" if Washington was accepted as a spokesman for all Negroes.

The deficit that DuBois identified has continued to plague African Americans right up to the present. Consequently, anyone who aspires to genuine leadership must be prepared to endure a rigorous screening process. (Or else so bamboozle the mainstream media that pundits routinely refer to you as a "black leader" even though you have no recognizable or measurable constituency, just leather lungs and a preoccupation with the first-person singular pronoun.) Obama complicated the usual protocols by stating from the outset of his presidential campaign that he aimed to represent all Americans. (Complexity ensued despite Chisholm and Jackson having made similar claims during their own runs.) As subsequent events made clear, his "improbable journey" would have been impossible without the wholehearted support of black voters. Still, Obama's unconventional origins challenged both black and white notions of black leadership, albeit in varying degrees.

Blacks' alleged hostility toward Obama seems to have been mischaracterized and overestimated from the outset.

Writing in the *Los Angeles Times,* the scholar Louis Chude-Sokei argued, "Among African-Americans, discussions about his racial identity typically vacillate between the ideologically charged options of 'black' versus 'not black enough' or between 'black' and 'black, but not like us.'" In the *Columbia Journalism Review,* Satta Sarmah confidently noted, "Those inside and outside of the black community have questioned Obama's racial identity. As the son of an African immigrant, Obama is not directly linked to the history of black enslavement in America, a fact that makes some blacks view him as more of an outsider." It's true that an occasional op-ed column (two? three?) raised such questions, but "some" and "among African-Americans" suggest a widespread suspicion that was never manifested. "Among African-Americans" I encountered, not one objected to Obama's own insistence that "I self-identify as African-American. That's how I'm treated and that's how I'm viewed, and I'm proud of it." Most discussions of him revealed attitudes that were initially noncommittal yet open-minded and revolved around two questions: (1) Did he have even a remote chance of attracting substantial white support? and (2) If he got close to victory, would he survive?

Inexplicably, it was members of the white punditocracy who often expressed weirdly confused ideas about Obama's racial identity. In the *New York Times,* Scott L. Malcolmson earlier had declared Obama "not black in the usual way." The *New Republic's* Noam Scheiber had judged him "not stereotypically African-American" (ouch). Steve Kroft of *60 Minutes,* perhaps unaware of mirrors in the Obama residence or given pause by the example of Tiger Woods, asked the candidate why he considered himself black. Jonathan Weisman of the *Washington Post* expressed during an online chat his belief that Obama is "more white than black, beyond skin color." (Weisman later apologized and acknowledged, correctly, that his comment was "really stupid" and "insensitive.")

Perhaps writing ironically, Peter Beinart of the *New Republic* contrasted Obama's suitability to represent the interests of African Americans with that of Al Sharpton. The latter's 2004 presidential campaign, although usually worth mentioning only as a curiosity or footnote, had made him "president of black America," according to Beinart. That would have been news to "black America": Sharpton failed to win even South Carolina, where nearly 50 percent of registered Democrats are black.

Mainstream journalists also may have been confused by instances in which blacks internalized racist stereotypes so deeply that their language betrayed them. If only James Baldwin were alive to help us make sense of Jesse Jackson's seeing Obama's unwillingness to be "all over Jena" as "acting white." The arrest of six black youths in that Louisiana town, in Jackson's view, was "a defining moment, just like Selma was a defining moment."

His predictable hyperbole aside, Jackson's criticism carried little weight—mostly because he was trying to force a twenty-first-century peg into a twentieth-century hole. Obama's swelling support showed that the vast majority of black voters handled the paradigm shift without stumbling. Nor, unlike the mainstream media, were they startled by any aspect of Obama's speech or conduct. They actually found him familiar, because, as the black journalist Ta-Nehisi Coates pointed out in *Time* magazine, "African-Americans meet other intelligent, articulate African-Americans all the time."

As much as black secular sermonizers speak truth to power, they must also be counted on to dispense constructive criticism to African Americans. Calls for responsibility or adherence to, in King's memorable words, "the high planes of dignity and discipline" are so closely woven into the tradition of black advocacy that attempts to categorize

African American leadership rhetoric as dependent upon grievance and victimology seem both curious and bizarre.

As far back as 1843, the pastor-activist Henry Highland Garnet articulated a strain of tough-love discourse that accepted no excuses whatsoever for black behavior that failed to meet the highest standards. Whereas modern professional opinionators often try to link such talk to conservative philosophies, the historical record reveals no opposition between insistence on excellence and black progressivism. For Garnet and his allies, excellence was itself a potent form of resistance. Nothing—not even chains—should hinder a black man from doing his best. "Your condition does not absolve you from your moral obligation," he told his enslaved brethren. "Therefore it is your solemn and imperative duty to use every means, both moral, intellectual, and physical, that promises success."

If any single concept spanned the range of black activism, thought, and rhetoric, it was—and continues to be—the "imperative duty" outlined by Garnet. For example, although they disagreed far more than they agreed, Booker T. Washington and W. E. B. DuBois found common ground in seeing the urgent need for resourceful effort. Washington warned his fellows against permitting "our grievances to overshadow our opportunities." DuBois asserted that "the responsibility for their own social regeneration ought to be placed largely upon the shoulders of the Negro people."

Similarly, Malcolm X and Martin Luther King were not so far apart where such ideas were concerned.

"We have to get together and remove the evils, the vices, alcoholism, drug addiction, and other evils that are destroying the moral fiber of our community. We ourselves have to lift the level of our community, the standard of our community to a higher level," Malcolm insisted in "The Ballot or the Bullet," an oft-quoted 1964 speech given after his ouster from the Nation of Islam. Three years earlier, King had told his own congregation, "We know that there are many things wrong in the white world. But there are many things wrong in the black world, too. We can't keep on blaming the white man. There are many things we must do for ourselves. . . . I know the situation is responsible for a lot of it, but do you know that Negroes are 10 percent of the population of St. Louis and are responsible for 58 percent of its crimes? We've got to face that. And we have to do something about our moral standards."

Obama's comments leading up to his presidential candidacy fit easily in line with such criticism. Consider these remarks, for example, less than a year after his 2004 convention debut, to an NAACP Freedom Fund Dinner in Detroit: "Our grandparents used to tell us that being Black means you have to work twice as hard to succeed in life. And so I ask today, can we honestly say our kids are working twice as hard as the kids in India and China who are graduating ahead of us, with better test scores and the tools they need to kick our butts on the job market? Can we honestly say our teachers are working twice as hard, or our parents?"

DuBois, in particular, usually attached such observations to the inequalities that made uniform black excellence so difficult to achieve. Black responsibility "must carry with it a grant of power," he said in a 1903 speech, "Training Negroes for Social Power." "Responsibility without power is a mockery and a farce."

Obama, too, has insisted that black failure be considered in a wider context, one that is not victimology-centered but simply tells the full story. In the Philadelphia address he suggested that we need to "remind ourselves that so many of the disparities that exist in the African-American community today can be directly traced to inequalities passed on from an earlier generation that suffered under the brutal legacy of slavery and Jim Crow."

Bill Cosby's controversial 2004 address commemorating the fiftieth anniversary of *Brown v. Board of Education* fits comfortably into the tough-love oratorical tradition. Echoing the King sermon quoted above, Cosby pointed to black misconduct as an especially damaging obstacle to black progress. "It's not what they're doing to us," he argued. "It's what we're not doing."

While few disagreed with Cosby's central premise, some observers (including myself) took issue with his insistence that "the lower economic and lower middle economic people are not holding up their end in this deal."

Cosby seemed to overlook middle-class and wealthy blacks' wanton indulgence in aspects of dysfunction, including adultery, domestic abuse, absentee fatherhood, and failure to pay child support. As DuBois and others have put forth, casting excessive blame on the less educated and economically disadvantaged allows successful blacks to hide their obligations to their brethren behind by-the-bootstrap myths of self-propelled ascent. In a speech delivered in 1934 on the day he resigned from the NAACP, DuBois outlined the consequences of such mythmaking in apocalyptic terms. "If the leading Negro classes cannot assume and bear the uplift of their own proletariat," he said, "they are doomed for all time." During his campaign, Obama managed to elude any whiff of bourgeois disdain. Jesse Jackson may have accused Obama of "talking down to black people," but examination of his speeches turns up no evidence of condescension.

Inevitably, the brand of constructive criticism favored by African American secular sermonizers has included an overt hostility toward self-pity—in blacks, whites, individuals, or the country itself. Again, Douglass established the tradition. He concluded his Fourth of July speech with a rejection of gloom. "Notwithstanding the dark picture I have this day presented, of the state of the nation, I do not despair of this country," he said. He pointed to technological advancements, "the genius of American institutions," and the spread of intelligence to "the darkest corners of the globe" as reasons for hope. DuBois later echoed Douglass's line of thinking but was less concerned with the rewards of optimism than with the potentially harmful consequences of self-pity. For him, as he told one unfortunate correspondent in 1905, despair was neither responsible nor representative. "How any human being whose wonderful fortune it is to live in the 20th century should under ordinarily fair advantages despair of life is almost unbelievable," he wrote. "And if in addition to this that person is, as I am, of Negro lineage, with the hopes and yearnings of hundreds of millions of human souls dependent in some degree on her striving, then her bitterness amounts to crime."

Arguments against despondency may have peaked in the speeches and sermons of King, who seldom failed to include a call for pressing on against all odds, for hewing "out of the mountain of despair a stone of hope." Obama's oft-quoted rebuttals to charges of naïveté ("I'm not talking about blind optimism," "there's nothing false about hope") obviously derive from King's example. But they probably owe just as much to the sermons of Jeremiah Wright, which also incorporate nonscriptural allusions, discussions of literature and music, and overt intellectual explorations. "The Audacity to Hope," Wright's 1988 sermon that inspired the title of Obama's second book (and some of the best lines in his 2004 keynote), begins with a meditation on a Victorian painting by George Frederic Watts, expands into an examination of the biblical story of Hannah, and sifts through the lyrics of an African American spiritual about faith in things unseen.

"There may not be any visible sign of a change in your individual situation, whatever your private hell is," Wright told his congregation. "But that's just the horizontal level. Keep the vertical level intact, like Hannah. You may, like the African slaves, be able to sing, 'Over my head I hear music in the air. Over my head I hear music in the air. Over my head I hear music in the air. There must be a God somewhere.'" Lean, elegant, powerful, and precise, Wright's sermon eloquently demonstrates that few philosophical threads weave so sturdily through black public rhetoric as radical optimism.

In a political context, encouragement must also include a call for purposeful decision and an acknowledgment that—amid the praying and rejoicing—there is work to be done. King frequently reminded his followers that they had "a long way to go." Barbara Jordan declared her fellow citizens "willing to suffer the discomfort of change."

Obama's 2005 Freedom Fund speech also took note of the tribulations along the path to full equality. "The road we have taken to this point has not been easy," he acknowledged before taking up a phrase that would become a staple. "But then again, the road to change never is."

For King, the road led to a Promised Land where white children and black children could sit together side by side. In Obama's modern, mostly secular take, the climb to the mountaintop incorporates "a journey that will bring a new and better day to America" in which the Promised Land shimmers in the glow of Perfect Union. The latter phrase is often associated with the "race" speech, but Obama had made it part of his repertoire as early as 2002. In the speech he delivered that year against the war in Iraq, he spoke of the Civil War as a sacrifice made by multitudes so "that we could begin to perfect this union."

King's best-known antiwar address was his speech against the Vietnam conflict at New York's Riverside Church delivered exactly one year before his death. He acknowledged that the price of peace was always high and sometimes bloody but had to be paid nonetheless. "Now let us begin," he said. "Now let us rededicate ourselves to the long and bitter, but beautiful, struggle for a new world." While Obama's campaign announcement often is, understandably, compared to Abraham Lincoln's arrival on the national stage, I was struck by how closely his call for civic participation aligned with King's address at Riverside. "Together, starting today," Obama concluded, "let us finish the work that needs to be done, and usher in a new birth of freedom on this Earth." By the time he accepted his party's nomination in August, he was still talking about the labor ahead but in more prosaic terms. "Let us begin the work together," he said. "Let us unite in common effort to chart a new course for America."

The conciliatory element, like the others described

above, is by no means limited to African American oratory. Obama's predecessors in the black rhetorical tradition often referred to the heritage of mainstream American rhetoric—its commonalities and its contradictions—in their own speeches. Those speakers' invocations of the secular scriptures, discussed above, not only commented both subtly and overtly on the divisions that have thwarted all Americans through the years—but claimed a place for the orators themselves in the nation's mainstream intellectual lineage.

Certain mainstream figures, such as Lincoln, a giant of American rhetoric, continue to influence black speechmaking. For example, Coretta Scott King spoke of her husband trying to "echo some of the Lincolnian language" when preparing to speak at the March on Washington. Barbara Jordan ended her 1976 keynote with a powerful quote from Lincoln: "As I would not be a slave, so I would not be a master. This expresses my idea of Democracy. Whatever differs from this, to the extent of the difference, is no Democracy." Obama has often borrowed imagery and language from Lincoln, and, perhaps audaciously, has not discouraged others from making a connection. While it may be hubristic to seek comparison with a president generally regarded as one of our best, Obama can reasonably claim to feel kinship with Lincoln's desire to bridge seemingly irreconcilable differences. And he seems to have had this idea before seriously considering a quest for the presidency. His keynote declaration, "we worship an awesome God in the blue states, and we don't like federal agents poking around in our libraries in the red states," clearly echoes Lincoln's Second Inaugural Address in which he said of Northerners and Southerners, "Both read the same Bible and pray to the same God, and each invokes His aid against the other."

But the conciliatory impulse resonates through black rhetoric quite compellingly on its own as well and needn't always be traced to "outside" influences. Even Malcolm X, who seemed to revel in confrontation, sought to reassure his audiences that they were all in the struggle together. This is especially true of the post-Mecca Malcolm, who demonstrated a greater appreciation of peace. "I'm not anti-Democrat, I'm not anti-Republican, I'm not anti-anything," he insisted. "I'm just questioning their sincerity, and some of the strategy that they've been using on our people by promising them promises that they don't intend to keep." Like King, he just wanted the government to be true to what it said on paper.

King, of course, was far more consistent in expressing a desire to build consensus. In 1963 he called for "trustful give and take on both sides." In 1967 he argued, "it helps to see the enemy's point of view." Obama's career-long tendency to build coalitions by reaching "across the aisle" to his Republican counterparts can, in some respects, be seen as a logical extension of King's call for give-and-take. "I am obligated to try to see the world through George Bush's eyes, no matter how much I may disagree with him," Obama wrote in

The Audacity of Hope. Rhetorical traditions aside, any liberal candidate who hopes to attract supporters beyond her base and thereby gain a reasonable chance at victory must include bridge-building phrases in her campaign language. (Alliances across race and interests have been neither desirable nor necessary for Republican candidates of the past several decades.) Shirley Chisholm showed that she realized this when she refused to be categorized as either the blacks' candidate or the women's candidate. Jesse Jackson, often maligned as a champion of grievance politics, acknowledged as much in 1984, when he called for Americans to "forgive each other, redeem each other, regroup, and move on."

Obama said as much during his remarks on the final primary night, June 3, 2008. He encouraged voters to avoid another election marred by partisan mudslinging: "We may call ourselves Democrats and Republicans, but we are Americans first. We are always Americans first."

He undoubtedly realized that he was, in some ways, preaching to the converted. The seeds of such a remarkable conversion were probably planted back in the days of Frederick Douglass and James Rapier, when they mesmerized skeptical whites with forceful eloquence utterly devoid of "plantation speech." They took root, however tentatively, when Martin Luther King and others spoke truth to power in unassailable terms. They began to blossom on the night the first black congresswoman from the South shared her impressions of the Constitution.

She received thousands of letters in response to her remarks, and the majority of them were positive. One in particular is especially useful here. "You have changed the minds of myself, my wife, our relatives, and all our friends, for the good of our country," its author confessed. "Before we watched you on TV we thought only a man should be the president but all of us will vote for you or any lady or black man or lady."

If he hasn't already, Barack Obama should offer humble thanks in memory of Barbara Jordan.

CHAPTER 6
Brothers from Other Planets

IN A SCENE in *Undercover Brother*, the title character suggests to his ally Conspiracy Brother (Dave Chappelle) that he relax and watch a movie. Conspiracy Brother reacts with disbelief.

"A movie? So I can fall in love with some cute black man that teaches white people everything they know about the shrimp industry before they kill him thirty minutes into the movie?"

He's talking about Pvt. Benjamin Buford "Bubba" Blue, the kindhearted, doomed war buddy of Tom Hanks in the 1994 film *Forrest Gump*. Ably played by Mykelti

Williamson, Bubba was warmhearted, generous—and destined to die before moviegoers' popcorn cooled. He was what knowledgeable film buffs often call a "Magic Negro." Usually such characters exist solely to assist a white protagonist in the pursuit of a goal (true love, say, or career success, or mastery of a sport). Unlike Bubba, they don't always die (those that do are sometimes known as "Expendable Negroes," once a staple of slasher and disaster films). Magic Negroes were seldom discussed outside black conversations until Rita Kempley, a white film critic, wrote an essay about them in the *Washington Post* in 2003. She observed, "It isn't that the actors or the roles aren't likable, valuable or redemptive, but they are without interior lives. For the most part, they materialize only to rescue the better-drawn white characters."

Kempley traces Magic Negroes back to the late 1950s, "around the time Sidney Poitier sacrifices himself to save Tony Curtis in 'The Defiant Ones.'" In my view, Noah Cullen, the character Poitier plays in that film, doesn't really qualify as a Magic Negro. Such characters usually choose to keep their emotions hidden by either a placid, inscrutable facade or a deceptive grin. Not so for Cullen. "I ain't gettin' mad," he tells Joker, the escaped jailbird played by Curtis. "I been mad all my nat'chul life."

But there is no question that Poitier often played Magic Negroes. Kempley quotes film historian Thomas Cripps, who offered a killer assessment that rings painfully true. "Sidney Poitier spent his whole career in this position,"

Cripps said. "Sidney actually carried the cross for Jesus in 'The Greatest Story Ever Told.'"

Mention the phrase at an African American cocktail party and names of actors, characters, and movies will fly fast and furiously. Homer Smith in *Lilies of the Field*. Mother Abigail in Stephen King's *The Stand*. John Coffey in Stephen King's *The Green Mile*. Dick Hallorann in Stephen King's *The Shining*. (King's reliance on Magic Negroes, often to great effect, is itself a subject worthy of lengthy examination.) Whoopi Goldberg in *Ghost*. Whoopi Goldberg in *Clara's Heart*. Hollywood has supplied Magic Negroes for almost as long as the movie industry has existed and gives no hint of stopping. Consider this observation from an A. O. Scott review of *The Secret Life of Bees:* "the film becomes a familiar and tired fable of black selflessness, in which African-Americans take time out from their struggle against oppression to lift the battered self-esteem of white people who have the good sense not to be snarling bigots. Even Ms. [Dakota] Fanning, weeping on cue and looking uncomfortable otherwise, seems a little abashed that the movie, in the end, has to be all about her." That review appeared in the *New York Times* on October 17, 2008.

It was watching such movies that led Ariel Dorfman, a Chilean novelist, to tell Kempley, "I sense that maybe deep inside, mainstream Americans somehow expect those who come from the margins will save them emotionally and intellectually."

A similar perception seemed to fuel David Ehrenstein's

op-ed column describing Obama's emergence as a political variation on white Americans' need for Magic Negroes. Writing in the *Los Angeles Times,* Ehrenstein argued, "He's there to assuage white 'guilt' (i.e., the minimal discomfort they feel) over the role of slavery and racial segregation in American history, while replacing stereotypes of a dangerous, highly sexualized black man with a benign figure for whom interracial sexual congress holds no interest." His essay appeared in March 2007, probably too early to note the ways in which Obama's emergence challenged some basic aspects of the Magic Negro archetype while sustaining others. Over time, Obama's opponents not only declined to replace his traditionally "dangerous" attributes (e.g., his sexual attractiveness) but also implicated the "magic" ones —his extraordinary eloquence, for example—as the very source of his potential to harm. It was perhaps also too early to anticipate how often considerations of Obama's "magic" qualities (such as leadership skills) accompanied suggestions regarding his sexual ones (such as Sarah Silverman's Great Schlep video, Obama Girl, Hot Chicks Dig Obama, and the *Nation* sex column).

Also, in stark contrast to having no past, Obama had perhaps the most candidly revealed (and thereafter, thoroughly scrutinized) personal history of any candidate in the race.

An African American himself, Ehrenstein expressed sympathy for Obama's struggles with observers who questioned his "authenticity." Those who raised such questions, he contended, regarded men like Al Sharpton and Snoop Dogg as "genuine" exemplars of blackness.

Radio talk-show host Rush Limbaugh, missing Ehrenstein's points entirely, responded with a musical parody aimed less at Obama than at Sharpton. Paul Shanklin, a Limbaugh collaborator, based the melody for "Barack the Magic Negro" on "Puff the Magic Dragon." Singing in a voice intended to resemble Sharpton's, he lamented the rise of a black political figure who was not from the "'hood" and was loved by the media. It was dumb and poorly executed to be sure, but worst of all, it obscured the relevant questions Ehrenstein had stirred up about the pitfalls of black exceptionalism and the right of black Americans to, in DuBois's words, find and commission their own leaders. Ehrenstein was right to point out the enduring desire of white Americans "for a noble, healing Negro." Also worth exploring is the degree to which black Americans desire, to use a less provocative phrase, an African American able to build strong alliances from unlikely forces. By the fall of 2008, as his general-election victory approached, Obama seemed poised to exploit an old stereotype even as he subverted it.

As a cultural fixture, Magic Negroes go way back beyond *The Defiant Ones*. Uncle Tom, Harriet Beecher Stowe's famous 1851 creation, must certainly be listed near the front of the line. Tall, powerfully built, and dedicated to a life in chains, Tom was designed to expose the moral failure of slavery while reassuring whites afraid of potential black violence. He prayed for his captors' souls even as they tortured him to death. Contrary to Ehrenstein's definition, Tom was not meant to assuage white guilt; he was intended instead to prod their consciences and provoke them to meaningful action. This was also true of Madison Washington, a Magic Negro at the center of Frederick Douglass's 1853 novella, *The Heroic Slave*. Douglass was even more explicit than Stowe when describing his "tall, symmetrical" protagonist's physical gifts, including his lionlike strength and arms of "polished iron." Washington was intelligent, born to lead, and as capable on land as he was at sea, and his encounters with whites left them in awe. They were awestruck but not afraid, because they regarded him as an "exception" to the general rule of black ignorance—a rule that, in their view, emancipation would have been powerless to affect.

While Magic Negroes often have no backstories in movies, they usually do in literature. Jim, Huck Finn's friend and one of the best-known and controversial Magic Negroes, discussed his wife and children at every opportunity. After proving his bravery and cleverness, he, too, earned his badge of exceptionalism. Over time, Huck found himself marveling that his companion had an "uncommon level head, for a nigger."

On the silver screen, as Ehrenstein suggested, Magic Negroes tend to "walk out of the mists." This is certainly true of the characters Poitier played in *Lilies of the Field* and *A Patch of Blue*. In the former, he drives up to a remote desert convent in search of water. Intent on just "passing through," Homer Smith has little to say about where he's been or where he's headed. But the Mother Superior who encounters him believes she has all the details she needs. "God is good," she says, staring at him. "He has sent me a big strong man."

The nuns need Smith to design and build a chapel, a task that requires more than just strength. "There are three ingredients to a job like this," he tells them. "First, you need a plan. Two, you need labor, and three, you need materials." Convinced of Smith's resourcefulness, Mother Maria needs no more proof that her desert wanderer is heaven sent. Homer, a Baptist, is unable to convince Mother Maria that his brand of Christianity is legitimate. But the construction skills of this noble Negro are sufficient to overcome any doubts she may have about his religious beliefs. She accepts him anyway. "He is not of our faith," she tells the tiny congregation, "but he was sent by our God who is the God of all faiths."

Similarly, a sense that Obama is a man of destiny, recently emerged from "out of the mists" to helm our complicated Republic, permeated much talk of his suitability for the presidency. As with Homer Smith, Obama's perceived construction skills—needed to rebuild the economy and other national infrastructures—dispelled lingering doubts about his faith, background, and motives. As November 4 approached, even jaded observers understood that nothing short of magic could win Obama endorsements from the *Chicago Tribune* and the *Los Angeles Times*. After all, the *Tribune* had never given its blessing to a Democratic candidate. Ever. In 161 years. The *Los Angeles Times,* its corporate sibling, hadn't endorsed any candidate for president since 1972. Just as Homer built a chapel from adobe, wood, strategy, and the applied labor of a multiracial coalition, Obama amassed a veritable tower of media support. By October 17, he had earned fifty-one newspaper endorsements to McCain's sixteen. The *Tribune* expressed "tremendous confidence in his intellectual rigor, his moral compass and his ability to make sound, thoughtful, careful decisions." "He is a consensus builder," the *Los Angeles Times* declared. "He represents the nation as it is, and as it aspires to be."

———

Two years after *Lilies,* as Gordon Ralfe in *A Patch of Blue,* Poitier pops up in the park just as young Selina D'Arcey needs a hand. He soon transforms her from a plain girl to a beautiful one with one simple gift: a pair of sunglasses.

"Now you're a very pretty girl."

"Pretty? Me?"

"Yeah, no sign of a scar. Your face looks perfect."

"Perfect? You're pulling my leg."

"No, I mean it."

"All because of these glasses? Sounds like magic."

"Yes it is. Kind of magic."

In his column, Ehrenstein compared Obama to a comic-book superhero, "there to help, out of the sheer goodness of a heart we need not know or understand." Several Magic Negro characters fit into that category. Rechristened "super-duper magical Negroes" by Spike Lee in 2001, they include John Coffey, the dim-witted, life-giving giant played by Michael Clarke Duncan in *The Green Mile,* Will Smith's mystical title character in *The Legend of Bagger Vance,* and my personal favorite, Woody Strode as Hank Lawson in *The Last Voyage.* That terror-at-sea flick was released in 1960, just a few years before Homer Smith brought his angel-on-wheels act to Arizona. Robert Stack and Dorothy Malone star as a loving couple taking a cruise to Japan. When a fire breaks out in the engine room, the sailors go into action. Lawson, the tallest and most muscular sailor aboard, soon appears, naked to the waist. He remains that way for the entire film. Lawson pulls away from the firefighting to assist Stack, whose wife has become trapped beneath heavy debris. Unlike John Coffey, Lawson is a giant with a brain. While helping Stack carry a two-hundred-pound tank up a flight of stairs, he explains how oxygen and acetylene can be combined to make a torch that will free Malone. During one extraordinary scene, Lawson keeps watch over Malone while her husband attends to their young daughter. Malone asks the noble stranger to kill her and end the family's misery. "I know it's a terrible thing to ask," she says, "but you could help me." Lawson declines, dismissing her entreaties as "crazy talk." Later, as water floods the sinking ship, Stack urges Lawson to board a lifeboat.

With a steady gaze—and in the glorious Standard English he's used for the entire film—Lawson refuses: "You can't get rid of me, sir, until your wife is out."

Lawson keeps his word, making sure the couple escapes the ship just before it goes under. He is the last man to board the last lifeboat.

Although Bagger Vance, like Lawson, is obviously as intelligent as the whites around him (if not more so), he is a much more problematic character. He walks out of the Savannah woods one shadowy night, carrying a suitcase and a penchant for platitudes. He apparently has arrived to carry clubs for Rannulph Junuh, played by Matt Damon, the town's golden boy gone to seed, in a high-stakes golf tournament. All he wants for his trouble, he says, is five dollars. While working with Damon he demonstrates his remarkable talent for weather predictions and golf-course measurement. He also shares such pearls of wisdom as "the rhythm of the game just like the rhythm of life" and "Golf course put folk through a lot of punishment. It lives and breathes just like us."

Vance is a backwoods Buddhist, one part Yoda, one part Huck Finn. His tutelage of Damon brings to mind a wrinkled old Jedi putting headstrong Luke Skywalker through his paces.

"You can't see that flag as some dragon you got to slay," he advises. "You have to look with soft eyes. See the place where the tides, the seasons, and the turning of the earth all come together, where everything becomes one. You got to seek that place with your soul."

At first I thought Vance was like Snuffleupagus used to be on *Sesame Street,* a figment of Big Bird's imagination that only the giant canary could see. I was reassured when other townsfolk interacted with him—albeit with a color-blind courtesy that defied belief. Clearly Bagger Vance's South was not the same place Noah Cullen pledged to avoid in *The Defiant Ones.*

"I'm a strange colored man in a white South town," Cullen said. "How long before you think they pick me up?" Bagger Vance is also a strange colored man in a white South town. But his burg is a postwar multiracial utopia miraculously devoid of "colored" water fountains, whites-only locker rooms, and, apparently, a local chapter of the Ku Klux Klan.

"They were hanging 'em high in Georgia then," Spike Lee has said. "If Bagger Vance really did have magical powers, wouldn't he help out his brothers? Do you really think his number-one concern would be helping Matt Damon with his golf swing?"

The film was a free-ranging adaptation of the *Bhagavad-*

Gita, which explains Vance's godlike talents. But that fact doesn't answer Lee's pointed and entirely reasonable questions. And Lee's concerns accurately reflect issues weighed by African Americans who have already expressed their unconditional support of Obama. Now that the brother had conclusively demonstrated his immense skills, would he use his powers for good?

Responding to the particular expectations of African American voters doesn't necessarily conflict with the needs of white Americans. But doing so will inevitably perturb some mainstream citizens who do indeed regard Obama as a real-life version of a Magic Negro. They will count on him to repay their loyalty by nurturing the perception that he belongs to them and them alone. In his book *Black Planet,* David Shields reflects on such presumptions. "Black men, and how we expect them somehow to redeem our pale white lives," he muses.

Never mind that Obama has spoken clearly against such notions throughout the campaign. In *The Audacity of Hope,* he suggests that his resistance to such ideas is a consequence of both politics and biology. "I've never had the option of restricting my loyalties on the basis of race, or measuring my worth on the basis of tribe," he writes.

Shields implies that basketball star Gary Payton fulfilled the role of a Magic Negro for SuperSonics fans during his glory years in Seattle. "We worship Gary Payton because he seems to be a brother from another planet," Shields writes.

He is referring to John Sayles's 1984 film, *The Brother from Another Planet,* starring Joe Morton as the quirky hero. As it happens, Brother, as he is known throughout the film, is an iconic Magic Negro who has frequently evoked comparisons to Obama.

"Obama takes on a Christlike quality for lots of people, especially white people," Jack Shafer wrote in Slate. "Obama has a talent for extending forgiveness to the guilty and the anxious without requiring an apology from them first. Go forth and sin no more, he almost says, and never mind the reparations. No wonder they call him the brother from another planet."

Unlike Bagger Vance, who exists to redeem white people and white people only, dark, silent Brother shares his gifts with everyone and especially those most in need. Having escaped bondage on his home planet (yes, apparently blacks have been slaves throughout the universe), he crash-lands at Ellis Island, absorbs the psychic anguish of that place, then tries to make a home in Harlem. He fixes machines, touches hearts, and fights a one-man war on drugs. He has a healing touch, can leap great distances, and is conveniently mute. This enables him to get along with all types. In the bar he frequents, Brother sits with two white tourists who've gotten lost on the way to a self-actualization conference. They find that a brief audience with him is a roughly equal if not superior activity; through his silent empathy they arrive at knowledge of their true selves.

"I didn't want to be like Ernie Banks," the first tourist confides. "I wanted to *be* Ernie Banks. It never dawned on me that he was black. I was seven years old. He was Ernie Banks. He was my hero."

Brother listens in silence, and the tourist responds emotionally. "If people would sit down and talk like this more often," he says.

"Communication," the second tourist interjects. "That's what it's all about."

Brother has a similar effect on his fellow blacks. Malverne, the honey-voiced singer with whom he has an affair, says, "How come I like you so much? You could be anybody."

In bed with his lover, Brother's unusual background makes him exotic, seductive. Like Superman, another alien who crashed to earth, his mysterious nature makes him lovable even though the earthlings he meets may believe that he's ultimately unknowable.

The overlapping tropes of Obama's atypical heritage and the super-duper Magical Negro played out in both favorable and hostile responses to his candidacy. On a collectible T-shirt designed by legendary comic-book artist Alex Ross, Obama appears as a brown-skinned Clark Kent, shedding the garb of an ordinary mortal to reveal the insignia emblazoned on his chest: a bright red *O*, done up superstyle.

Captain Obama is a superhero with extraordinary powers and unprecedented idealism dedicated to hope, freedom, and change for the American people. The origin story of Captain Obama was that he was born Barack Obama on the planet Earth. As a child he started to display superhuman abilities, which upon reaching maturity he resolved to use for good, not evil. Keeping his secret identity hidden, Barack Obama lives among the humans as a social activist and community organizer, helping the impoverished and speaking for the unheard voices of America.

ImagineGate Toys and Funko Toys have teamed up to bring you the first Barack Obama Superhero Toy!

As much as anybody, Obama knew that the mythology growing up around him yielded a vulnerable underside too tempting for his opponents to bypass. That has always been the case with Magic Negroes—or, more accurately, anyone perceived as such. As it has been with fictional figures ("The familiar objection to the novel is that Uncle Tom is too good," Alfred Kazin noted about *Uncle Tom's Cabin*), so it has been with real-life heroes. Writing in *Newsweek,* Jonathan Alter surmised that stories about Obama's alleged connections with unsavory figures "even if discredited, offer voters a permission slip to vote against a man they consider, in the title words of a John Sayles movie, 'The Brother from Another Planet.'"

Right up until his victory, Obama sought to defuse the hagiography with jokes and assertions of humility. At the Alfred E. Smith Foundation dinner in mid-October, he "denied" being born in a manger. "I was actually born," he said, "on Krypton and sent here by my father Jor-El to save the Planet Earth." From day one, he had forcefully described his quest as a collective effort. "That is why this campaign can't only be about me," he said on that blustery day in Springfield. "It must be about us—it must be about what we can do together." On August 28, when he at last accepted his party's nomination, he told his audience, "What the naysayers don't understand is that this election has never been about me. It's been about you."

It had been a refrain during the long, tempestuous run, but everyone didn't buy it. Joe Klein of *Time* magazine found the line "not just maddeningly vague but also disingenuous: the campaign is entirely about Obama and his ability to inspire. Rather than focusing on any specific issue or cause—other than an amorphous desire for change—the message is becoming dangerously self-referential. The Obama campaign all too often is about how wonderful the Obama campaign is." In the *New York Times,* Paul Krugman had warned, "the Obama campaign seems dangerously close to becoming a cult of personality."

Members of the public also took it upon themselves to monitor the media's growing chorus of praise. "I was very disappointed in your fawning cover story on Obama's campaign team," a reader complained in a letter to *Newsweek* last June. "Somehow you forgot to mention that Obama walks on water and heals the sick with his touch. . . . You can do better. If not, then you need to just openly join Obama's campaign and stop passing yourself off as a newsmagazine."

At their best, Klein and Krugman were part of a group of engaged and often sympathetic critics, more intent on keeping Obama honest than on throwing him off course. Their conscientious, civil objections seemed mere puffery when compared with some of the vitriol unleashed from anti-Obama factions.

"You could be anybody," said the Brother from Another Planet's lover. As appealing and charismatic as the Magic Negro can appear to be, he is ultimately an enigma. His depiction in books and movies suggests that it is possible to love and admire him, but the affection one feels toward him is best tempered with suspicion, if not outright fear. "The black body has, of course, been demonized in Western culture: represented as ogreish, coarse, and highly, menacingly sexualized," the African American scholar Henry Louis Gates Jr. has noted. "But the black body has also been valorized, represented, perceived as darkly alluring—still highly, menacingly sexualized but, well, in a good way. And this, historically, is its ambiguous dual role in Western civilization."

Through no fault of the Magic Negro's, those ambiguities create a convenient path straight from the world of slander and rumor to, in Alfred Kazin's pungent phrase, "the doltish open mouth of the public." In Obama's case, that conduit enabled the sly insertion of innuendo:

> Steve Kroft: You said you take Senator Obama at his word that he's not a Muslim. You don't believe that he's a Muslim. . . .
>
> Hillary Clinton: No. There is nothing to base that on. As far as I know.

And it permitted John McCain to pose disingenuous questions . . .

> All people want to know is: What has this man ever actually accomplished in government? What does he plan for America? In short, who is Barack Obama?

. . . and leave his followers to fill in the blanks:

"Terrorist!" "Arab!" "Liar!" "Kill him!"

Then there were the television ads promoting the argument that Obama was too "risky" to serve as president. Obama's vast war chest enabled him to greatly outspend McCain for TV ads, but his spots differed dramatically in tone. A study by the Wisconsin Advertising Project at the University of Wisconsin-Madison determined that roughly one-third of Obama's ads attacked McCain directly while virtually all of McCain's attacked Obama. Gary Kamiya, writing in Salon, contended that the subliminal message of all McCain's spots was that Obama is "scary, black, unknown, black, alien, black, un-American, black." The Brother from Another Planet, Osama bin Laden, and Willie Horton, all Photoshopped into one dark, horrifying monster.

In his column, E. J. Dionne commented on "a deep frustration on the right with Obama's enthusiasm for shutting down the culture wars of the 1960s." In truth, however, the few embers left from those conflicts were effectively doused long before most of us knew who Obama was. The Baby Boomers still stuck on "the decline of civilization," "us versus them," and "sticking it to the man" would do well to consult with the Millennials in their midst. And if the Millennials aren't too busy participating in social networks revolving around politics, environmentalism, and other issues that they find far more important, they might put down their iPods long enough to tell the Boomers to take a look around. Consider, they might say: 50 Cent sells vitamin water. Ice Cube stars in warm family comedies. Ice-T, once reviled for a song called "Cop Killer," is now best known for starring as a wizened detective on *Law and Order*. When allegedly bloodthirsty misogynists—and others supposedly responsible for the collapse of American values—are welcome in your living room, a black man in the Oval Office shouldn't even be worth a second thought.

For all his vaunted fix-it skills and his wondrous facility for patching old hurts, the Brother from Another Planet can only do so much alone. As with any gifted individual, "transcendence" for him becomes possible only with the help of a band of dedicated, like-minded allies. Throughout his campaign, Obama spoke on the need for collective movement. "Contrary to the claims of some of my critics, black and white, I have never been so naive as to believe that we can get beyond our racial divisions in a single election cycle, or with a single candidacy—particularly a candidacy as imperfect as my own," he declared in his "race" speech delivered in Philadelphia. But the nature of his media coverage often threatened to reshape the narrative of the campaign into the storied quest of a single noble Negro.

Barack's wife, Michelle, did her best to humanize the candidate's persona. Her early comments at fund-raisers attempted to reconcile his public and private images: "There's Barack Obama the phenomenon. He's an amazing orator, *Harvard Law Review,* or whatever it was, law professor, bestselling author, Grammy winner. Pretty amazing, right?

"And then there's the Barack Obama that lives with me in my house, and that guy's a little less impressive. For some reason this guy still can't manage to put the butter up when he makes toast, secure the bread so that it doesn't get stale, and his five-year-old is still better at making the bed than he is."

Maureen Dowd, a *New York Times* columnist, disapproved of Michelle Obama's commentary, which, she wrote, "rests on the presumption that we see him as a god." Dowd shared her concerns in May 2007. By then, many of her fellow journalists had convincingly demonstrated that such presumptions weren't entirely off the mark. So many gushy profiles and news articles had already appeared that Slate had launched Obama Messiah Watch, "a periodic inquiry into whether Barack Obama is the son of God." Slate writer Timothy Noah explained that the feature would "spotlight gratuitously adoring biographical details that appear in newspaper, television, and magazine profiles of the junior U.S. senator from Illinois, best-selling author, *Harvard Law Review* editor, *Men's Vogue* cover model, Grammy winner, and exploratory presidential candidate. The objective is not to insult Obama, but rather to restore a little rationality to the coverage of his potential candidacy."

A year after the feature's debut, the effusive praise had become a deluge of hyperbole. In February 2008, MSNBC's Chris Matthews told the *New York Observer,* "I've been following politics since I was about 5. I've never seen anything like this. This is bigger than Kennedy. . . . This is the New Testament."

And that was hardly the most enthusiastic comment, merely a representative one. Journalists, celebrities, and people on the street strove to outpace each other in the volume and vigor of their praise. Oprah, unsurprisingly, set a very high bar while campaigning for her fellow Chicagoan in South Carolina. "He is the One," she proclaimed. (The depth of feeling conveyed in her voice made it clear that the *O* should be capitalized, as it is on her magazine.)

Over time the love just grew, despite the sniping and slandering from the opposing camp. Sidney Poitier carried the cross for Jesus; if Obama had been cast in a remake of *The Greatest Story Ever Told* after his third debate with McCain, he'd have been the one wearing the crown of thorns.

"I think it's fair to say that no modern American politician, not even Ronald Reagan, has entered the arena with as much symbolic, even messianic, baggage as Obama has," Bruce Handy observed in a *New York Times* review of children's books about Obama. Yes, that's right: children's books so worshipful that they turned a critic's mind toward thoughts of scripture and salvation—a miracle for sure.

Joe Klein had seen it coming. "The expectations are ridiculous," he wrote in October 2006. "He transcends the racial divide so effortlessly that it seems reasonable to expect that he can bridge all the other divisions—and answer all the impossible questions—plaguing American public life."

Of course, Mrs. Obama had seen it sooner. (Some estimates credit Oprah with winning about a million votes for Obama; it's possible that Michelle brought him even more, especially among black women voters.) As bright, clean, and articulate as her husband, she knew his enormous popularity would raise questions about "the appropriateness of princely leadership in a democratic cause," as Taylor Branch once put it. She also knew that Martin Luther King Jr., much admired among his people in his day, had nonetheless been derisively called "De Lawd" behind his back. If folks got the notion that Barack was getting a big head, they might agree on the need to take him down a peg. It was something she had to address, Maureen Dowd be damned. The point, she told *USA Today,* was to let people know that he was not the "next messiah, who's going to fix it all." The paper quoted her telling a New Hampshire audience, "He is going to stumble . . . make mistakes and say things you don't agree with."

The Obamas may have found even more agreement than they expected among black voters, who demonstrated a degree of pragmatism that appeared to startle the pundit class. Like Amiri Baraka at Georgetown, black voters understood the difference between the United States and the Urban League. "Even if we get 30 percent from Obama, we're not going to get that from anybody else," a black Chicagoan explained to the *Washington Post* nearly a month before Obama announced his candidacy. "From white folks, we might get 10 percent. What I worry about is that we might want too much from him. It's not about us out here; it's about everybody."

Various photos of Obama, his wife, and children, circu-
lated via e-mail, provided one telling measure of African
Americans' interest in his improbable journey. Especially
popular were images of Barack and Michelle together. For
some stretches of the campaign, hardly a day passed when
I didn't receive a picture or series of pictures of the couple,
complete with emotional testimonies on the cheering effect
of seeing such a dynamic—and dynamically black—pair.

Occasionally included among the inspirational portraits
were images of a gaunt, fatigued Barack Obama, shots that
provided some sense of the campaign's steep toll. One such
photo appeared in my in-box on the night of the third debate. It showed Obama squatting in a stairwell. The collar
of his business shirt was unbuttoned, his sleeves were rolled
up at the elbow, and he held a notepad of some sort in his
hands. He was looking up toward a group of people vaguely
outlined on the nearby stairs, but his expression suggested a
desire to be somewhere else. The sender had written above
the photo: What must it feel like? To carry the hopes and
dreams of an entire race of people on your shoulders?

The question, motivated by compassion, spoke to the
enormous burden that the historic candidacy had imposed.
More than any other black candidate's quest for the presidency, Obama's had acquired a symbolism and intensity
of feeling that cut across disparate categories of African
American life. The photo and its bold caption recalled a
scene in Obama's memoir in which he decompressed fol-

lowing a wild party. A female friend had chewed him out, challenged his integrity and questioned his values. Instead of reclining in a stairwell, he slumped on a sofa and lit a cigarette. He was depressed and angry about the way his friend had torn into him as if, he recalled, "I was somehow responsible for the fate of the entire black race."

In the half-light of the stairwell, Obama suggested to me the unlikeliest of Magic Negroes: Bagger Vance, who inexplicably concealed his godliness beneath a cloak of humility. When asked who he was, Bagger replied, "Just me. Just a man trying to find somewhere to rest his tired feet."

CHAPTER 7   Fired Up

ALL WE SEE now is the same tired old men who keep trucking down front to give us the same old songs and dances," Shirley Chisholm lamented back in 1970, two years before her historic run. She believed the country was suffering from a lack of responsible leadership.

"It may be that the only hope is with the younger generation," she wrote in *Unbought and Unbossed,* her first memoir. "If I can relate to them, give them some kind of focus, make them believe that this country can still become the America that it should have been, I could be content."

She likely would have found some measure of satisfaction in the focused, faithful young people who surfaced in great numbers to support Barack Obama's candidacy. I'm certain she'd be pleased with students like David J. Walker. I became aware of him after one of his professors told me about the young man's involvement in bringing Obama to his school in 2006.

Two years later, I met with David on campus, amid a bustling health fair taking place at the Martin Luther King student center at Bowie State University, a historically black institution about seventeen miles outside the nation's capital. At an array of tables and booths, health-care professionals offered back rubs and blood pressure measurements, solicited blood donors, touted the New Minority Male Health Project, and dispensed advice on quitting tobacco. The atmosphere was energetic, busy, crackling with intelligence, and the room was populated, surprisingly, by a sizable contingent of male students.

They were the kind of black kids we often overlook, the ones not seen on newscasts in crime reports. They were kids with solid high school grades and the moxie to go to college while holding down at least one job. Lower middle-class, probably, and definitely not wealthy. Privileged, you might say, but not pampered. I never leave a school like Bowie State without being impressed by the students I've encountered, but also feeling as if my generation has failed them in some way; that whatever we're doing for them is not enough.

But that may be cynicism talking—the world-weary distrust of good fortune typical of many black folks my age.

Maybe the worst thing we could do would be to pass that glass-half-empty view on to these hardworking, hopeful young people.

I may be worrying too much, because there are some indications that my generation's gloomy attitude is rolling right off their backs. In their book on the Millennials, Morley Winograd and Michael D. Hais write that young Americans like these are "an exceptionally accomplished, positive, upbeat, and optimistic generation."

That seemed to be the case at Bowie State. I saw few sullen expressions, even with final exams looming. I saw young men in slacks and buttoned-down shirts (and even one necktie) alongside young men in oversize polos, baggy jeans, and baseball caps turned sideways—every one of them carrying a backpack or a bundle of books.

Jazz-themed posters shared wall space with posters listing the theater department's past and upcoming productions ("New Play Festival," *The Katrina Monologues*). Above the booth featuring representatives from the Alcohol, Tobacco and Other Drug Prevention Center, a huge portrait of Reverend King dominated the wall. (It showed him in his signature pensive pose, index finger extended along his determined jawline, his eyes apparently aimed at some far-off Promised Land.

I waited for Walker near a coffee kiosk where the barista had just celebrated her fifty-first birthday and called every student "baby."

Walker was a junior, twenty-three years old when we met. Originally from southeast Texas, he's the son of a military veteran who now works as a government contractor in Afghanistan. He's lived a number of places and spent his first two years of high school in Germany. He's almost tall, just under six feet, and very slender. He's a political science major. When he was asked why he became involved in politics, his initial answers differed little from the responses we've seen from other young people. Many of them are concerned with America's standing abroad. Just as Lincoln worried that slavery would deprive "our republican example of its just influence in the world," Obama's youthful supporters believe that ending the ongoing wars in Afghanistan and Iraq would help repair our nation's sullied reputation. Jessica Alba, the beautiful actress who starred in a risqué voter-registration campaign called "Only You Can Silence Yourself," spoke on the subject during a cameo in Will.i.am's "We Are the Ones" video. "I would like the rest of the world to think highly of our amazing country," she said. Sarah Silverman, the controversial young comic who often wrestles with racial stereotypes in her work, expressed the same idea, albeit in her typically salty language. In a video promoting "The Great Schlep," an effort to enlist Jewish support for Obama, she called him "probably our last hope of ending this country's reputation as the a——holes of the universe."

(Three weeks before the general election, the *New Yorker* atoned for its earlier stumble by endorsing Obama over McCain. Its editors also pointed to the Democrat as a possible solution to the United States' faltering international reputation: "Obama has inspired many Americans in part because he holds up a mirror to their idealism. His election would do no less—and likely more—overseas.")

Personal experience shaped Walker's desire to improve what others think of our country. "Right now the world perceives the United States of America as some huge imperialistic power," he said. "When I lived overseas for two years I saw the drastic change in how we're looked at from when Clinton was in to when Bush got in for the first time. I witnessed how the dollar began to slowly lose its strength."

Listening to Walker, I easily envisioned him summing up arguments in front of a jury, or whispering sage advice to a witness at a legislative hearing. But his ambitions extend beyond the walls of a courtroom or the lawmaking chambers on Capitol Hill. "My dream is to work in the State Department and help reshape our nation's image," he said.

After his return to the States, Walker decided to get involved in politics. By September 2006 he had become an intern with the Maryland Democratic Party. He was assigned the mundane tasks associated with such lowly posts, including inputting numbers from polls and answering phones. "It was boring," he recalled. "I wanted to be out there calling the shots."

His energy and university contacts soon won him a

promotion to campus coordinator and second assistant to the state party chairman. Not long after, he overheard plans for an ambitious event. "They were looking to do a huge rally in Prince George's County for all of the Democratic candidates that were running that year. I jumped in the conversation."

Walker secured the cooperation of Bowie State and co-sponsorship commitments from organizations on campus. He agreed to a number of preconditions, including making sure the school's name wasn't included on the promotional materials and inviting the Republican Party to convene a similar event on campus grounds. "I contacted the Republicans," he said. "I got a response two weeks later saying 'Thanks for your interest, here's a bumper sticker.'"

He spent a hectic ten days meeting with campus officials such as the athletic director and the chief of police—and coordinating logistics with party operatives. Three days before the event, he found out that Obama had agreed to appear. "About five hours later, that's when it hit: I was like, wow, this is the man that has a better chance of being in the White House than Jesse Jackson or any other person of color has ever had, so I got nervous."

Interest in the rally multiplied dramatically. On the day of the event, fifteen hundred people squeezed into the university gym. "It was just crazy," Walker told me. "I had people from CNN, NBC, Fox News, WPGC, and WHUR begging me to get them backstage."

That area had no shortage of party dignitaries, including Martin O'Malley and Anthony Brown, soon to be elected Maryland's governor and lieutenant governor, respectively, and Sen. Barbara Mikulski.

"I'm sitting with the provost," Walker recalled. "Next thing you know, someone says, 'Barack Obama's in the building,' so everybody starts getting nervous. I was speechless. Here he comes, whips around the corner, and every jaw hits the ground at the same time. Every student back there, our jaws just hit the ground."

Walker described a scene in which the senator paused to shake every hand and smiled through a series of group pictures. Every candidate for state office wanted a moment with Obama and, according to Walker, he obliged each of them. Finally it was time to enter the gym. "We got in the procession order and everything just took off. We walked out of the greenroom and walked out there. We walked into the gym. It was so loud and bright. I mean, wow! I will never forget that day.

"He had that gym packed. People were in the lobby fighting to get in. The excitement of it was . . . I still can't describe it. It was just that overwhelming, even remembering it now."

The scene Walker described sounded exactly like reports I'd read elsewhere of college students' reactions to Obama. And, more astutely than any candidate before him, Obama had set up a campaign structure designed to maximize support by turning their admiration to registration and, finally, to actually voting on election day.

Last June, Obama told *Time* magazine, "We just had some incredibly creative young people who got involved and what I think we did well was give them a lot of latitude to experiment and try new things and to put some serious resources into it."

All the way to November 4, his team reached out to voters via e-mail, Facebook, YouTube, and other Internet modes of contact. Whereas politicians and pollsters have never been able to sufficiently gauge young voters' preferences because few surveys include cell-phone users, Obama made his choice of running mate accessible to cell-phone users first.

His August 23 text-message announcement seemed to be conceived with his youthful supporters in mind. In 2006 the nonpartisan Public Interest Research Group (PIRG) conducted a study of young voters and found they were more than 4 percent more likely to vote if they received a text message reminder the day before. With nearly 90 percent of Americans ages eighteen to twenty-four owning a cell phone, that's a lot of potential votes.

In mid-October, Obama took his campaign to the world of video games. His team bought ads in nine games published by Electronic Arts, an industry giant. They appeared in Madden NFL 09, NBA Live 08, and other favorites of males aged eighteen to thirty-four. According to *PC World,* "at some point as you're cruising around a race track or slamming padded hockey players into plexiglass, pow, there's Obama, with the message that early voting's underway." The magazine called the ad buy the first time a presidential candidate "has gone all out to capture the youth vote by taking the campaign to the masses."

All the more evidence that the Millennials are "the most target marketed generation in history, the most connected. They are all about building community," said Julia Cohen. A longtime activist and member of the Progressive Happy Hour Crew, a Washington, D.C., group that canvassed Virginia on behalf of Obama, Cohen told the *Huffington Post,* "Obama is reaching them: text, mobile phones. . . . Obama understands this generation, and his campaign is providing young voters with the tools to build communities, clans, family."

These communities have taken forms that political operatives may not have envisioned before. At the University of Richmond, housing officers distribute a questionnaire to incoming freshmen in order to match them with suitable roommates. Michael J. Gaynor, an undergraduate who helped sift through the responses, told the *Chronicle of Higher Education,* "I had a stack of about 10 people who put, 'Has to like Obama.' "

They probably had no difficulty finding a suitable roommate. In August, a Greenberg/Democracy Corps poll of six hundred young people ages eighteen to twenty-nine found strong support for Obama across several categories of registered voters: 80 percent of young people of color, 68 percent of students, and 62 percent of unmarried women indicated their intention to vote for the Democratic nominee. Overall, Obama led McCain 57 to 29 percent, and 56 percent of those surveyed agreed with the statement "I am more involved in this election than in previous elections." The poll's authors determined that McCain's attempts to belittle Obama as a shallow celebrity had "not proven effective because young people's support and enthusiasm for Obama is based on something real. They sincerely believe he can change things."

Youthful voters had exceeded previous tallies in numerous states during primary season. Sujatha Jahagirdar of Student PIRG's New Voters Project told the *Washington Post* that turnout had doubled in New Hampshire, tripled in Iowa, and quadrupled in Tennessee. Perhaps the most dramatic indication of Obama's appeal was his endorsement by Lauren Wolfe and Awais Khaleel, president and vice president of College Democrats of America. The pair chose Obama on May 13, 2008, after soliciting opinions via a YouTube video they had posted less than three weeks before. The duo reported receiving more than five thousand e-mails and more than five hundred YouTube comments— and their video was viewed more than twenty-one thousand times. Quite naturally, they announced their decision to back Obama on YouTube. Among the many respondents was "Karla," a student at San Diego State University. *Washington Post* writer Jose Antonio Vargas called her response "arguably the longest 44-second video" in the history of the site. His partial transcription read: "Please, please, please vote for Obama. Vote Obama. Pleeeaaassse. It would mean a lot to me and trust me when I say this: a lot, a lot, like, hundreds of thousands of people would thank you for it. Like, seriously, okay I'm making this too long. Bye. Thank you. Please vote Obama. Obama. Bama. Bama. Barack Obama."

I asked David Walker why he thought young people responded so warmly to Obama. After all, I reminded him, Obama's not an athlete or an entertainer but a politician, and he's as old as their parents.

He smiled patiently and shook his head. "He's different from all of them," he explained. "In some shape or form, he's different from the average senator, the average person on Capitol Hill. I still can't tell you what it is. When that man opens his mouth, people listen. People listen."

Walker went on to compare Obama to Jay-Z, a connection that, as I mentioned earlier, gave me pause.

I was still adjusting to Obama's appearance in the same magazines that popular entertainers such as Jay-Z typically graced. I feared it cheapened him somehow, that it risked letting glitz overshadow substance. Why should the first black president of the *Harvard Law Review,* a man whom one law professor had described as perhaps the most gifted

student she'd ever taught, be on the cover of *Men's Vogue,
Rolling Stone,* and *Vibe*?

Danyel Smith, the talented editor of *Vibe,* put it in perspective for me during an interview with the Associated
Press. She said she put Obama on the cover "because for
the first time since *Vibe* was launched in 1993, a political
figure has burst on the scene and fired up young people in
a major way. Because regardless of who wins the election,
the Senator will have inspired many new voters to go to the
polls. Because Obama is frank, brilliant, vibrant, and not
cynical—all things that make him a perfect *Vibe* cover."
Editors like Smith, whose livelihoods depend on know-
ing young people's interests and desires, had seen the truth
of David Walker's observation: when Obama opened his
mouth, their readers listened.

Walker told me that he came from a family of Democrats but he was still concerned about all his relatives showing up at the polls. "I told my mom, if you love me, you will
go and vote. You will make sure everybody in the family is
out there to vote for this man."

The Great Schlep project revolved around a similar impulse. Sponsored by the Jewish Council for
Education and Research, a pro-Obama political action committee, the campaign encouraged young Jews to journey to
Florida over Columbus Day weekend. While there, they
were to visit their grandparents and convince them to vote
for Obama. In exchange, suggested Sarah Silverman in the

campaign video, the grandparents would get another visit. If they declined to vote for Obama, they wouldn't see their grandchildren again for an entire year.

"If Barack Obama doesn't become the next president of the United States, I'm going to blame the Jews," Silverman began. "I know you're saying, 'Oh my God, Sarah, I can't believe you're saying this. Jews are the most liberal, scrappy, civil rightsy people there are.' Yes, that's true, but you're forgetting a whole large group of Jews who are not that way."

Silverman's monologue stuck closely to the kind of challenging material that has earned her notoriety. With cheery mock sincerity, she identified some of the things young black men have in common with Jewish grandmothers, including a love for tracksuits, Cadillacs, "things and bling and money and stuff." In addition to being the chosen candidate, she assured viewers, Obama was "circum-supersized." Fearless, irreverent, and occasionally tasteless, the video seemed well tailored to inspire and entertain a new generation of voters, few of whom appear to have their elders' racial (and sexual) hang-ups.

It was not exactly the kind of material the Obama team could manufacture but, like Will.i.am's videos, was precisely the kind of viral media that took the campaign into unexpected directions and yielded unexpected rewards. "Many analysts in both parties believe that racial attitudes in this country are changing at a breakneck pace, particularly among younger voters, making it risky to impose models from even four years ago on this unusual election," the *New York Times* noted last April. The Great Schlep perfectly illustrated the speed of change.

Their elders may be thrown off balance by the dramatic societal transformations taking place, but young voters are steady on their feet because they've never known anything else. While their parents and grandparents remember *Guess Who's Coming to Dinner* and Petula Clark touching Harry Belafonte's arm, the new generation made box-office hits of interracial fare like *Save the Last Dance*. Having grown up on *Sesame Street,* Nickelodeon, MTV, and the Disney Family Channel, they've known mixed-race casts since birth and cut their teeth on shows that consistently depict parents—of all ethnicities—as clueless and hopelessly out of touch. The bands and performers they favor, from the Neptunes to M.I.A. to the Gym Class Heroes, are as likely to have diverse lineups as not. The authors they admire— writers such as Junot Diaz, Jhumpa Lahiri, and Jonathan Lethem—also span the racial gamut. The lifelong immersion of mainstream American youth in multicolored pop culture has resulted in some fascinating developments. Nearly ten years ago, in a *Newsweek* piece taking note of black optimism, Ellis Cose attributed a new African American attitude to the expanded national imagination, which "freely celebrates the appeal and accomplishments of African-Americans. Michael Jordan, Lauryn Hill, Colin Powell—pick your icon; if you are touched at all by

American culture your idol is likely to be black. There have always been black successes and superstar achievers, but never before has black been quite so beautiful to so many admirers of every hue."

Cose quotes one black man who asks, "When did you ever think you would see black men as the heroes of white children?"

That, it turns out, was just the beginning.

A February 2008 *Jet* magazine article reported on the findings of a Stanford University research project on American heroes. In a nationwide survey of two thousand high school juniors and seniors, researchers asked students to list the ten most famous people in American history, from Christopher Columbus to the present. (Presidents and first ladies were excluded.) The top three finishers were (1) Martin Luther King Jr., (2) Rosa Parks, and (3) Harriet Tubman. One other black notable, Oprah Winfrey, came in seventh.

"We were interested in popular historical consciousness," Sam Wineburg, lead author of the study, told *Jet*. "There has been a very significant shift. The symbolic father and mother of the American story are now Dr. Martin Luther King Jr. and Rosa Parks."

Would these shifts be reflected in the general election? Or would the lingering specter of racism prove an irresistible force? Up to election day, pundits and political scientists dissected and reassembled the arguments, then divided them up again. Back and forth they went, scattering talk of Bradley effects and "reverse" Bradleys, all of which simply revealed the uncertainties swirling in the air.

Such deliberations often offered a sober antidote to the optimism accompanying Obama's long slog toward the finish. Six months before the election, a trio of *Newsweek* writers had reflected, "it is discouraging to think that a small minority of racists could make the difference."

That same month, the *New York Times*'s Frank Rich boldly asserted, "There is little evidence to suggest that there are enough racists of any class in America, let alone in swing states, to determine the results come fall."

Oh yeah? "There are a lot fewer bigots than there were 50 years ago, but that doesn't mean there's only a few bigots," Stanford political scientist Paul Sniderman told the Associated Press last September. And so it went.

Then the dispiriting footage from Sarah Palin's incendiary rallies began to make the rounds. Almost reflexively, many of us noted the essentially monochromatic character of her audiences and chalked up the violent sentiments expressed to the rantings of a tragically misinformed minority.

Snoop Dogg, a gangsta rapper known more for his violent, embarrassing lyrics than for his political commentary, nonetheless aptly summed up the fears of many observers. He told *Newsweek*'s Allison Samuels, "People that I know have never cared about politics are registering to vote this time: gang members, ex-cons, you name it. I hate to see a lot of that hope go down the drain, and if he loses, it will."

As might be expected, younger voters were far less perturbed. Ali Close, a twenty-year-old Utah resident, shook off her family's Republican habits to support Obama. "I have not heard of his race being an issue except in the respect that 'OK, this is the first time,'" she told the *Salt Lake* (City) *Tribune*. Obama "definitely excites youth," she added, "and I don't believe McCain does."

Billy Mills, Democratic Party chairman in Onslow, North Carolina, noticed similar indications in his neck of the woods. He told the *Washington Post*, "I'd say the older forces of the county, the retirees, they're still Republican. But there's a lot of younger folks that see it differently and that have registered Democratic as a result of their interest in Obama. This has been the biggest movement that I've seen in a long time."

In *The Audacity of Hope*, Obama writes of crisscrossing Illinois and discovering that much of what the state's residents believed "seemed to hold constant across race, religion, and class." If the attitudes of his youthful supporters were any evidence, those beliefs would be sufficiently common to elevate him to the White House. More than with any presidential candidate before him, Obama's success or failure depended heavily on the strength, faith, and reliability of young America.

Kerry Washington, a lovely actress who campaigned

for Obama, had been one of the most thoughtful commentators in "We Are the Ones." "The thing that inspires me most about Barack Obama is that he really is going to be the president of the United States," she said. "He's not going to be the president of the top 10 percent or the president of the most powerful corporations or the president of the most powerful lobbyists. He's going to be our president. He's going to speak for us because we put him there."

Lauren Champaign, a twenty-one-year-old campaign worker in Charleston, South Carolina, told the *Washington Post* that she gave up a scholarship to Georgetown Law School to work for Obama. "That's how much I believe," she said.

Obama clearly derived part of his confidence from the demonstrated loyalty of supporters like Washington and Champaign. He told Jon Stewart of *The Daily Show,* "We're especially seeing a lot of young people and that is one of the things that's most exciting about the campaign is folks who haven't seen a lot of inspiration in politics most of their lives suddenly taking this seriously."

Inspiration is the key word for David Walker, the once and future diplomat from Bowie State. He told me, "Clinton said a lot of the stuff he says is just dreams, but the country is founded on dreams. Everything that inspires you to become something in life comes from a dream."

CHAPTER 8 The Tattered Veil

IN HIS MEMOIR, *Walking with the Wind,* John Lewis describes preparing for the March on Washington with Bayard Rustin, A. Philip Randolph, and the other civil rights leaders involved in the historic event. "While we were still at the Capitol, word came that the march had begun without us," Lewis wrote.

"'My God, they're *going,*' said Rustin, as we stepped outside the Capitol to see masses of people moving down the streets. 'We're supposed to be leading *them!*'"

"We were supposed to be the leaders of this march," Lewis recalled, "but the march was all around us, already taking off, already gone."

While the idea of these high-minded leaders, the vaunted vanguard of black America, scrambling to catch up with the streaming multitudes is in some ways comical, it's also instructive. It perfectly illustrates Doug Wilder's observation, "Times never change, but people do, and people are ahead of their leaders."

Perhaps no recent example demonstrates the truth of that maxim better than Obama's presidential campaign. After a slow start, the masses moved decisively. And the leaders—prominent black pastors, mayors, key members of the Congressional Black Caucus—scrambled to catch up. As Obama gained momentum, picking up as much as 90 percent of black voters in various districts, the leaders were forced to reassess their initial backing of Hillary Clinton. John Lewis was among those struggling to avoid waking up, as he put it, on "the wrong side of history."

Along with Rev. Joseph Lowery, former head of the Southern Christian Leadership Conference, and a few others, Doug Wilder was one of the black elder statesmen who embraced Obama early on. "I think Obama was right about not waiting for someone to tell him that it was his time," he said. "My feeling has always been that if a thing is right, the time is always right, and Obama is showing that as well as anyone could."

As might be expected, Lowery often expressed similar sentiments but in his typical pulpit-rattling style. In January 2008, for example, he proclaimed while others dithered: "No matter how much education they have, they never graduated from the slave mentality. The slave mentality compels us to say 'We can't win. We can't do.' Martin said the people who were saying 'later' were really saying 'never.' But the time to do right is always right now."

Wilder and Lowery's attitudes provided a sharp contrast to those of other black public figures, whose reactions ranged from reluctance to rejection. Al Sharpton fit into the first camp. He said that all the media hoopla surrounding Obama amounted to little more than sizzle, leaving him waiting to find out "where the meat is."

Andrew Young's comments placed him in the second group. Now in his late seventies, Young is a Clinton ally who earned his stripes as one of Martin Luther King's capable, trustworthy aides. In 1972, at age forty, he became the first black congressman from the South since Reconstruction. During a live television interview in December 2007, Young surprised audience members by suggesting that Obama was not yet ready for the nation's highest office. "Barack Obama does not have the support network yet to get to be president. He's smart, he's brilliant, but you can't be president alone."

Sharpton and Young are apples and oranges. What they had in common was a failure to anticipate Obama's arrival and subsequent appeal among African Americans. With his processed hair, lack of a measurable constituency, and talent for attracting the attention of clueless mainstream media, Sharpton brings to mind an astute passage from *Black Metropolis:* "Frustrated in their isolation from the main streams of American life, and in their impotence to control their fate decisively, Negroes tend to admire an aggressive Race Man even when his motives are suspect."

Where Sharpton built his reputation (such as it is) on bluster and threats, Young built his as the soft-spoken negotiator on King's team. With his emphasis on diplomacy and deal making over confrontation, he is in many ways a forerunner of the new black politician. More than many of his peers, he seemed to have a long-term view of black political progress. He had previously declined to see community activism and working within the system as inherently conflicting pursuits. Electoral politics, from Young's perspective, was "a way of sustaining what we had done and needed to do again, rather than as a deviation from our history of collective struggle." As mayor of Atlanta, he had courted white business leaders so aggressively that black critics charged him with neglecting issues of pressing concern to inner-city residents, such as rising crime.

But his initial objections to Obama seemed to stem less from philosophical disagreements than from loyalty to the Clintons. Young suggested that Obama would be better off running in 2016. Further, Young said, "I've talked to people in Chicago and they don't know anybody around him. To put a brother in there by himself is to set him up for crucifixion."

Young apparently needed to update his BlackBerry, for Obama was hardly by himself. His relationships with black executives such as Valerie Jarrett, CEO of the Habitat Company, and John Rogers, founder of Ariel Capital Management, among others, were well known. Jarrett eventually left her job to work on the campaign full-time. "Everybody said, 'He'll never be able to raise the money; he'll never be able to get an organization together; no one will come and work for him, all the other candidates have taken all the good people,'" Jarrett said. "But, you know, all our life people have been telling us you're not good enough, you're not ready, so don't even try."

Obama may have had such comments in mind when, in *The Audacity of Hope,* he described his generation of black professionals as rejecting "any limits to what they can achieve." Media accounts of his staff suggest that Obama's hires reflected that philosophy.

Writing in *Ebony* magazine, Sylvester Monroe debunked "false reports early in the campaign that there were no African-Americans in top campaign staff positions." He identified "more than two-dozen talented blacks in key slots that Obama has attracted from the ranks of the nation's best and brightest minds."

The "talented blacks" in Monroe's story tended to be in their thirties and forties, as young as, or younger than, Obama. One suspects they are part of the group Matt Bai discussed in an article for the *New York Times,* "Is Obama the End of Black Politics?" For the young African Americans he wrote about, "the resistance of the civil rights generation to Obama's candidacy signified the failure of their parents to come to terms, at the dusk of their lives, with the success of their own struggle—to embrace the idea that black politics might now be disappearing into American politics in the same way that the Irish and Italian machines long ago joined the political mainstream." Young, savvy black voters are likely to remember incumbent waffling in subsequent congressional contests; the efforts of the old black vanguard to keep their style of politics alive may actually have hastened its demise.

Members of the black right were equally unenthusiastic about Obama's campaign. In his book *A Bound Man,* Shelby Steele argued that Obama would fail in part because he couldn't criticize black achievement without bringing collective black scorn down on his head. "If, for example, Obama broke with this determinism by saying that blacks themselves were largely responsible for closing the academic achievement gap with whites," Steele wrote, "he would likely be seen as an Uncle Tom for letting whites 'off the hook.' So, in order to be black, he must pay tribute to a determinism that makes whites ultimately responsible for black uplift, even when it is obvious that only black responsibility will make a difference."

But Obama had broken with such "determinism" during his first national public appearance, his keynote speech at the 2004 Democratic convention: "Go into any inner city neighborhood, and folks will tell you that government alone can't teach our kids to learn; they know that parents have to teach, that children can't achieve unless we raise their expectations and turn off the television sets and eradicate the slander that says a black youth with a book is acting white. They know those things."

By June 2008, he was still hammering home that same message: "That's why so many children are growing up in front of the television. As fathers and parents, we've got to spend more time with them, and help them with their homework, and replace the video game or the remote control with a book once in a while. . . . It's up to us to set these high expectations. And that means meeting those expectations ourselves. That means setting examples of excellence in our own lives."

Jesse Jackson had shaken off those same alleged ideological shackles when he first ran in 1984. His advice to readers of *Ebony* after the campaign: "We cannot reach maturity if we watch five hours of TV at night and choose entertainment over education, or if we put cocaine in our membranes and our bodies are too weak and our minds too destroyed to make a contribution. We cannot just focus on opportunity; we must also focus on effort, and effort and character must be more dominant than opportunity."

Blacks not only declined to label Jackson an Uncle Tom but also turned out in even greater numbers to support him in 1988. Similarly, the young people who support Obama, both poor and prosperous, show no indication of meditating on the significance of Uncle Tomism. (Their cultural references are so modern, fluid, and ahistorical that many of them are probably unfamiliar with old Tom.) If anything, they see his comments as a prescription for success. Recall Jay-Z's remarks earlier: "What [Obama] represents is, we as a people are a part of the American Dream. The message is for a kid from Marcy projects right now to say, 'Maybe I can be the president.'"

Through the decades, *Ebony* has explored the possibility of an African American commander in chief with admirable, farsighted dedication. "We polled our readers in July 1983 asking whether a Black should run for president, and in October we gave their answer: a Black should run and the candidate should be the Rev. Jesse Jackson," the magazine's editors noted in a 1984 issue devoted to black politics. Jackson's subsequent campaigns, along with input from his son Jesse Jr., probably influenced his decision to give Obama his blessing early, in March 2007.

But his relationship with the campaign was problematic at best. In November 2007, a Jackson op-ed piece in the *Chicago Tribune* evaluated the Democratic candidates without mentioning Obama at all. Jackson faulted the entire lineup except John Edwards for failing to address "the separate and stark realities facing African-Americans." He and other left-leaning commentators urged Obama to keep pace with Edwards's overt populism. As Darryl Lorenzo Wellington pointed out in *Dissent* last fall, "the absence of emphatic anti-poverty advocacy remains a key distinction between the Obama campaign's 'change' message and the language associated with black protest movements, the Jesse Jackson campaigns or the NAACP." Of course, groups like the NAACP (and Jackson's erstwhile Rainbow Coalition) have specific constituencies with specific demands, and their leaders are chosen by internal deliberation or self-designation, not by the general acclaim of the ballot box.

Wilder had pointed out that distinction when he faced comparisons with Jackson during his own brief presidential campaign. "Jesse is an activist, perhaps the foremost activist of our time. I'm an elected official," he explained. "I have to work with more coalitions, tolerate more diverse viewpoints. It's not stellar, but it's more productive over the long run. We've just chosen different roads."

After Jesse Jackson's pointed omission of Obama, Jackson Jr. weighed in with his own op-ed. "I've been a witness to Obama's powerful, consistent and effective advocacy for social justice and economic inclusion," he testified. In what may have been a dig at the older generation, he added, "Obama has addressed many of the issues facing African Americans out of personal conviction, rather than political calculation."

Writing in the *Washington Post,* historian William Jelani Cobb argued that much of the criticism aimed at Obama amounted to "a kind of reverse affirmative action." While white Democratic candidates in previous campaigns, such as Gore and Kerry, escaped public scrutiny from black progressives, Obama, "a former civil rights attorney who has litigated employment and voting discrimination cases, has to pass a 'good faith' test."

If Jackson Sr. really believed there was more than one path to productive black leadership, his comments provided little indication. In July 2008, he was caught criticizing Obama over a live microphone. The candidate had been "talking down to black people," said Jackson, who also expressed a desire to manually castrate him. He apologized for those remarks, but Jackson Jr. stepped forward again to repudiate his father, this time in forceful fashion. His statement read, in part, "I'm deeply outraged and disappointed in Reverend Jackson's reckless statements about Senator Barack Obama. His divisive and demeaning comments about the presumptive Democratic nominee—and I believe the next president of the United States—contradict his inspiring and courageous career. . . . Reverend Jackson is my dad and I'll always love him. He should know how hard that I've worked for the last year and a half as a national co-chair of Barack Obama's presidential campaign. So, I thoroughly reject and repudiate his ugly rhetoric. He should keep hope alive and any personal attacks and insults to himself."

By now, the tension between Obama and Jackson—and their respective approaches—was commonly understood. In March, *Saturday Night Live* had aired "The Obama Files," an animated segment that showed Obama going to great lengths to escape association with Jackson and Sharpton. While both men were portrayed as eager to help the candidate, they were also depicted as foolish, ignorant, and out of touch. The animated version of Obama was so desperate to keep his distance from Sharpton that he had him outfitted with a collar that shocked him when he got too close. In a little more than four minutes, the spoof managed to be smart, cruel—and funny.

In Obama's view, real-life comparison to Sharpton and Jackson wasn't appropriate either. He told the *New York Times* last December that such discussions were untenable "because neither Rev. Jackson nor Rev. Sharpton is running for president of the United States. They are serving an important role as activists and catalysts but they're not trying to build a coalition to actually govern."

The increasingly feverish McCain-Palin ticket threw all manner of innuendos at Obama, hoping that something would stick. The candidate was busy rebutting and/or shrugging off the various accusations, and the last thing he needed was yet another headache caused by Jesse Jackson. Early in the race, Jackson had accused Obama of "acting white" in his response to the Jena Six controversy. Considering that outburst in conjunction with the *Tribune* op-ed and the castration episode, observers wondered if Jackson could possibly do anything else to derail Obama's march to victory. The answer, perhaps inevitably, was yes. A *New York Post* columnist reported that Jackson, speaking before a World Policy Forum held October 14 in France, suggested that an Obama presidency would put an end to excessive "Zionist" influence in American foreign policy. In a subsequent "clarification," Jackson repudiated the column and confirmed that he "has never had a conversation with Sen. Obama about Israel or the Middle East."

Obama's camp was again forced to issue a strong denial: "Rev. Jesse Jackson Sr. is not an adviser to the Obama campaign and is therefore in no position to interpret or share Barack Obama's views on Israel and foreign policy. As he has made clear throughout his career and throughout this campaign, Barack Obama has a fundamental commitment to a strong U.S.-Israel relationship, and he is advised by people like Dennis Ross, Daniel Kurtzer, Rep. Robert Wexler, Rep. Debbie Wasserman Schultz, and Senator Joe Biden who share that commitment." Although the cartoon Jackson and the live-action character were sometimes hard to tell apart, the latter proved much harder to get rid of.

For his part, Sharpton told the *New York Times* that Obama began his campaign as "the alternative to guys like me," as if black voters having a range of leadership styles to choose from—as opposed to having would-be leaders thrust upon them—was a bad thing. The continuing lack of rapport between the old guard and the new generation proved that DuBois was right when he argued that a group benefits most when "by search and criticism it finds and commissions its own leaders." Chris Rock had said as much during his 1999 "Bigger and Blacker" show, when he lamented, "we ain't had a black leader in a while. In a long time. Somebody that moves you. You know, we had Martin Luther King, Malcolm X—and ever since then, a bunch of substitute teachers." Evidently Obama was somebody that moved Rock, who became an active and vocal supporter of his campaign.

Dissatisfaction with the Jackson-Sharpton school of black spokesmanship is largely—and perhaps correctly—seen as a generational development. But there are signs that not just young African Americans are willing to consider the "shift in metaphors" that Obama has advocated. That shift, he said, requires democracy to be seen "not as a house to be built, but as a conversation to be had." That conversation should include people like Helen Francis Money Freeman Dennis, a ninety-year-old black woman with something on her mind. In a remarkable YouTube video, she is shown going to vote in the Pennsylvania primary last April. She says she is excited to support Obama because "he has a brain" and "looks like he could go somewhere." Dennis expressed little patience for blacks' earlier attempts to get to the White House. "We never had it come this close," she said. "We had 'em saying poetry and all that kind of crap. . . . Jesse sat up there saying all that doggone poetry and sing-song stuff. Ain't no substance to Jesse."

Obama has both substance and style, according to Colin Powell. On October 19, 2008, the retired general crossed party lines to endorse Obama's candidacy. His announcement on NBC's *Meet the Press* was as much a condemnation of widespread hostility toward Muslims as it was a statement of support for Obama. Accompanying Powell's denunciation of anti-Islamic attitudes, however, was a clear statement of praise for Obama. Powell said he'd studied Obama closely throughout the long campaign and, in his view, the Democratic nominee "demonstrated the kind of calm, patient, intellectual, steady approach to problem-solving that I think we need in this country."

James Baldwin allegedly once suggested a method by which younger black writers could replace their tenacious forebears. "The sons must slay the fathers," he is believed to have said. Politics is nearly as bloody a business as art, but changes in power needn't be so Oedipal. Powell's statement provided a clear sense of one generation peacefully passing the torch to another—and illuminated the succession issues that have long complicated traditional black leadership. Malcolm X left no trained apprentices behind; King's legacy, to his credit, included a sizable group of disciplined, experienced aides. If John Lewis, Stokely Carmichael, and other former leaders of SNCC trained a coterie of younger activists, the presence of their ideological descendants in contemporary leadership positions is hard to detect. Ditto for Jackson and Sharpton. As Joshua Alston noted in *Newsweek,* "Rather than taking the tools of the civil-rights movement—stirring rhetoric, symbolic unity, nonviolent resistance—and arming a new generation with them, Jackson and Sharpton have never let go."

Three weeks before the election, Atlanta journalist Maynard Eaton asked Jackson, sixty-seven, if he was "passing the torch" to Obama. He declined to answer the question directly. "Each of us must in our own day serve while the sun is still high," he replied. "Reagan became president twice, and he was older than I am now."

Ironically, Jackson's biological heir, Jesse Jr., has in common with Powell a belief that Obama is a "transformational figure." As such, Obama is poised not only to lead the country but also to help usher in forms of black leadership that will supplement rather than supplant the old ways of doing business. In late 2005, he told his biographer David Mendell, "I just think that I am the most prominent of a new generation of African-American voices. . . . I actually have felt very comfortable speaking on issues that are of particular importance to the African-American community, without losing focus on my primary task, which is to represent all the people of Illinois. And I haven't felt contradictions in that process."

Twenty-one years before Obama made those remarks, Eddie N. Williams and Milton D. Morris of the Joint Center for Political Studies outlined the future of black politics in remarkably similar terms. In an essay in *Ebony,* they predicted, "Black politics is likely to be transformed in other respects as well. One such transformation will probably be in the way Blacks formulate and articulate their goals. The dynamics of presidential politics—and increasingly politics at other levels as well—will require Blacks to forgo race-specific articulation of policy objectives in favor of broader objectives that encompass Black goals."

Obama, as he himself suggested, is at the center of such a transformation. But its roots are various and have been growing for some time. "I think we're going to think of ourselves as not only representing the black community, but representing everyone," said Alzo Reddick, a Democrat who worked on Wilder's campaign back in 1992. "To me, Wilder represented the future of America in terms of black politicians crossing over (to white voters)."

While the shift that Reddick described is easier said than done, it is being accomplished and has been under way at least since blacks were first elected mayor in major cities and certain black U.S. representatives were sent to Congress by majority white districts. While on occasion such blacks will certainly be accused of having divided loyalties (see Andrew Young, for example), they are far less apologetic in defending their "crossover" ambitions. Ralph Ellison wrote that the artist feels "a near-unresolvable conflict between his urge to leave his mark upon the world through art and his ties to his group and its claims upon him." Substitute *politician* for *artist,* and *politics* for *art,* and you have a pretty good idea of the pressures confronting the new generation.

Deval Patrick, governor of Massachusetts (the second

black, after Wilder, ever elected to such a post), was an early Obama supporter. He has felt the squeeze from black interest groups demanding more attention. "Sometimes I think advocates want one note from us. I think our experience in our lives and in our politics has been that there's much more than the one note—and sometimes a cacophony."

Michael Nutter, mayor of Philadelphia, backed Hillary Clinton during the primary campaign. Like Corey Booker in Newark and Obama on the national level, he has had his racial allegiances questioned on more than one occasion. But if he finds that discouraging, he isn't letting on. "I'm proud of the votes I received," he told the *New York Times*. "I'm proud I received the votes of the majority of the African-American community and the majority of the vote from the white community. But I never asked anybody to *give* me anything because I was black. I asked people to give me a chance because I thought I was the best."

In his book *Black Leadership*, the historian Manning Marable wrote that such leadership has traditionally revolved around a set of common pursuits, including "respect as human beings, unfettered participation in the economic and political life of this country, full civil liberties, and equal protection under the law." In the new American majority envisioned by Obama, Patrick, and their allies, those goals will continue to be pursued. What has changed is the fact that all African Americans no longer face the same set of common conditions. "Unfettered participation," for example, will not necessarily mean the same thing to Obama's daughters as it does to a young girl growing up in the Marcy projects.

Some observers fear that advocacy on behalf of that girl—and the other voiceless millions—is precisely where the new generation will falter. Old-school definitions of leadership seldom deviated from a model that looked out for the disadvantaged first. "Jackson is the voice of the poor, the disenchanted, the disillusioned," Shirley Chisholm once said of Jackson's campaign, "and that is exactly what I was." Indeed, Jackson was probably at his best when acting in that capacity, instead of, say, negotiating diversity agreements with Wall Street. His speech at the 1988 convention contains, for me, one of the finest examples of Jacksonian eloquence: "Every one of these funny labels they put on you, those of you who are watching this broadcast tonight in the projects, on the corners, I understand. Call you outcast, low down, you can't make it, you're nothing, you're from nobody, subclass, underclass; when you see Jesse Jackson, when my name goes in nomination, your name goes in nomination."

Obama claims to understand the importance of "representativeness" for black Americans but has always been careful to place it in a larger context. "For you as a presidential candidate to want to lead this country, you've got to speak to those who have been left out of the process," he has said. "Otherwise you can't make a claim to be representing all of America."

Frederick Douglass, who confidently spoke for all of his fellow black Americans, believed his role was to "agitate, agitate, agitate"—that is, to persuade those in power to govern the country fairly and conscientiously. Similarly, Reverend King operated from the belief that, in his words, "privileged groups seldom give up their privileges voluntarily" and therefore have to be shown that generosity is not only right but in their best interest. Obama, it is understood, aims to speak from the seat of power itself; no black voter could reasonably expect him to perform as agitator-in-chief. Instead, black communities' appointed agitators (many of whom will now hail from Obama's generation and will share some of his opinions and points of view) will approach him and expect an attentive audience. This will undoubtedly change the dynamics involved in speaking truth to power. As comedian Wanda Sykes put it, "You can't blame the man if you *are* the man." But the definition of "the man" is changing even as Obama takes on the mantle of national leadership. Will Obama be the man who can make things happen by snapping his fingers? More than a few black Americans believe, as Obama once overheard in a barbershop, that "whenever a black man gets into power, they gonna try and change the rules on him."

Or will he be the man as in the one responsible for everything negative—past and present—associated with the United States? Exactly how much of the government's institutional baggage Obama is expected to inherit remains to be determined.

The definition of black community is also in flux.

"I have called my community a world, and so its isolation made it," DuBois wrote in his *Autobiography*. "There was among us but a half-awakened common consciousness, sprung from common joy and grief, at burial, birth, or wedding; from a common hardship in poverty, poor land, and low wages; and, above all, from the sight of the Veil that hung between us and Opportunity."

If the Veil exists at all now, it's tattered and hanging by a thread. The isolation that DuBois described doesn't even apply to the poor anymore: many of them have access to cable television and, through libraries and other institutions, the Internet as well. While housing segregation is still widespread, general cultural isolation can only be self-imposed.

While some communities continue to be defined by those common hardships that DuBois mentioned, other communities have left those limitations far behind. Is a common blackness sufficient to bind these disparate groups? Do those aforementioned Marcy project kids belong to the same community as Gilbert Arenas? Black, twenty-five, and slated to make $14.5 million this year as an NBA All-Star, Arenas told the *Washington Post* he had no plans to vote. "It doesn't really matter who the president is," he said. "They say whatever they need to say to get in office."

The most effective spokesmen for these various and wildly different constituencies will rise organically from their memberships and surroundings, just as they did in the days of Martin Luther King Jr., John Lewis, and Fannie Lou Hamer. Advocacy organizations must also adjust to the modern era by using technology to further their activism, and many of them already are. As citizens whose needs and interests will overlap across communities, we must learn to rely on multiple channels to access change, in the same way one handles a remote-control device or a PDA. For assistance about an environmental concern, for example, we might turn to Van Jones's group Green For All; to combat those instances where institutional racism still rears its ugly head, we might look to the NAACP, where Ben Jealous has identified injustice as a primary concern. Ideally, leadership skills developed in certain interest groups could then be parlayed into elected offices and vice versa. The career path for a future leader might, like Obama's, begin in community service and lead to elected office—before returning to grassroots activism.

After Obama takes office, poor black people aren't going away. Neither are our other pressing problems, which span various income categories—the continuing spread of AIDS and other STDs; astronomical dropout, illiteracy, and incarceration rates; and out-of-wedlock births—they will still be around as well. Obama's rise doesn't spell the end of oppression, but it exposes the fallacy of referring to all black Americans as particularly oppressed or oppressed specifically because of their blackness. More than ever, we will be forced to look at these problems through new lenses. We have to avoid misguided wistfulness; we have to insist on looking forward. Otherwise our hidebound skepticism, which has yielded its own peculiar comforts, may leave us, in Obama's words, "entombed in nostalgia." If we willfully immerse ourselves in that imperfect past, then we have more in common than we ever dreamed with the stagnant, sputtering Pat Buchanans and Trent Lotts of the world, our bafflement matched only by the volume of our bellowing.

In *Dreams from My Father,* a man who knew Obama's dad tells Barack Jr. about the difficulties faced by educated Africans returning to their homeland: "Of course, when we returned we realized that our education did not always serve us so well. Or the people who had sent us. There was all this messy history to deal with." The same is true for Obama and the new generation of African American leaders that he represents. They are a fresh alternative offering exciting new options not only for black communities but also for the country at large. But they emerge even as age-old problems remain unaddressed and underlying injustices remain unpunished. Obama has promised that he—with our help—can deal with that messy history and make from it "a new kind of politics," something vibrant, powerful, and transcendent. "It will have to be constructed from the best of our traditions," he wrote in *The Audacity of Hope,* "and will have to account for the darker aspects of our past."

If practiced skillfully, Obama's formula could lead to the more perfect union we all hope for. The best we can do is hold him to it.

EPILOGUE The New Black, the New America

THE PROBLEM HERE is that few Americans know who and what they really are," Ralph Ellison observed in a 1970 *Time* magazine essay. He was referring to the nation's white majority, but he often made similar comments about the dark-skinned minorities living in their midst. Our differences, he suggested, led—paradoxically—to certain commonly held neuroses and uncertainties that prevented us from coming together, even though we knew that genuine unity was in all our best interests.

Ellison called on whites to recognize aspects of their behavior—usually gleaned from popular culture—that they picked up from blacks and other Americans. In those elements, he argued, were the keys to solving the riddles of American identity.

It was an argument that had been made before. In 1925 the philosopher Alain Locke had suggested that the modern black American—the New Negro—was "the augury of a new democracy in American culture." Locke's claim was an audacious one to make back then, but Obama's extraordinary ascent has given it the aura of prophecy.

"If there is anyone out there who still doubts that America is a place where all things are possible," declared Obama during his victory speech, "who still wonders if the dream of our founders is alive in our time, who still questions the power of our democracy, tonight is your answer."

Decades before Obama ever set foot on Harvard's storied campus, Locke flourished there. Initially, as a Harvard graduate and the nation's first black Rhodes scholar, he tried to bypass racial categorization as an act of will. "I am not a race problem," he declared in a 1907 letter to his mother. "I am Alain LeRoy Locke."

But the realities of American (and European) racism intruded on his ambitious plans. As a professor at Howard University and as editor of *The New Negro,* a landmark anthology of black art and culture, he responded by working to portray the emerging generation of black intellectuals in the best possible terms. A philosopher by training, Locke saw art as a way to foster understanding between ethnic groups and advance the acceptance of blacks into mainstream American society.

Locke wrote that the New Negro so defied simple description that he baffled not just race men but nearly everyone else as well. The few who readily grasped the New Negro's meaning were members of the younger generation, who were "vibrant with a new psychology" and whose awareness was proof of a "new spirit awake in the masses." These changes had taken place, Locke wrote, "under the very eyes of the professional observers."

But in Locke's view, "the thinking Negro" in the form of artists and intellectuals, such as Langston Hughes, W. E. B. DuBois, James Weldon Johnson, and Anne Spencer, confounded all the old ways of striving. As a result, they influenced in their fellow citizens "a sudden re-orientation of view."

Obama's victory has forced a similar change in perspective, not just in African American communities but also in the nation at large. He suggests a new kind of optimism that is at once defiant (in the face of challenging odds and dire circumstances) and patriotic (in which a desire to improve oneself becomes inseparable from a desire to contribute to the country's revival). "I can't help but *make* myself think more positively now," said Christine Cook, a black schoolteacher quoted in the *Chicago Tribune*.

Smart black people have never been invisible to other black people. Nor, of course, have they been invisible to whites, who have often chosen to see them as exceptions to a general rule of black ignorance and subpar intellectual performance. Black communities have also suffered weird internal neuroses regarding black brains. Smart black people have always been acknowledged and sometimes even admired. But, even in the nation's middle-class black meccas, being smart has seldom been widely promoted as a desirable lifestyle choice, especially among schoolchildren and adolescents. That's where the change that Obama has called for will begin to manifest immediately. Even in places where black pride has been defined by nihilism and the willingness to hide powerlessness behind a cloak of bluster, it will be fashionable to be brainy. On election night, in African-American communities across the country, smart became the new black.

"The intelligent Negro of today is resolved not to make discrimination an extenuation for his shortcomings in performance, individual or collective," Alain Locke wrote in 1925. "He is trying to hold himself at par, neither inflated by sentimental allowances nor depreciated by current social discounts. For this he must know himself and be known for precisely what he is." In his 2004 keynote convention speech, Obama touched on the danger of making excuses for black anti-intellectualism. That night in Boston he condemned "the slander that says a black youth with a book is acting white." Obama's achievement of the White House makes it easier to see—and believe—that a black youth with a book is, in fact, acting presidential.

We know that a few days of euphoria cannot undo nearly four hundred years of hateful inaccuracies. To paraphrase Bayard Rustin, we are aware of the folly in attempting to provide psychological solutions to problems that are profoundly economic. "But now," as Dana Hull observed in the *San Jose Mercury News*, "and for at least the next four years, the most quoted, photographed and broadcast face and voice will be that of a Harvard University–educated black man. It is the face Americans will turn to during national crises for information and reassurance. At the annual State of the Union address, it is a black man who will outline the goals and successes of the most powerful country on earth."

A black commander in chief who is also the nation's intellectual in chief will inspire African Americans not only to celebrate intelligence but also to expect nothing less.

We will demand intelligence from our pastors.

We will demand intelligence from our athletic stars.

We will demand intelligence from our entertainers.

We will demand intelligence from our politicians.

We will demand intelligence from our community activists.

We will demand intelligence from the various ethnic groups with which we share this nation.

We will demand intelligence from each other.

"The dogmas of the quiet past are inadequate to the stormy present. As our case is new, so we must think anew, and act anew."

Those words of Abraham Lincoln's neatly describe the actions of millions of voters on November 4, 2008. They apply especially to the white voters whose election day choices were made less predictable by fears of a Bradley effect. Such fears proved unfounded: The multitudes that Obama attracted in unlikely places like Iowa, Vermont, Indiana, and North Carolina turned out in droves to provide him with the biggest Democratic victory since Lyndon Johnson vanquished Barry Goldwater in 1964. The remnants of old-school racism that reared up in certain quarters prior to election day were not revealed as omens of a November surprise but exposed as the last gasps of a dying pathology.

In the end, it was about hope, not hate.

And also about intelligence. White voters ultimately "had to ask themselves if they wanted a really smart young black guy, or a stodgy old white guy from the same crowd who put us in this hole," Tina Davis told the *New York Times*. She is a white politician in a predominantly white Pennsylvania district that voted overwhelmingly for Obama. Perhaps the voters saw what Hendrik Hertzberg saw when he watched Obama deliver his "race" speech in Philadelphia. In Hertzberg's view, Obama "treated the American people as adults capable of complex thinking—as his equals, you might say."

Thanks to Obama's convincing, thorough demonstration of intelligence and verve, modern-day Jack Kerouacs in search of that elusive black magic may no longer walk the streets with kicks, darkness, and other abstractions dancing in their heads. Likely as not, they may come to associate blackness with brilliance, thoughtfulness, confidence, and radical optimism. There are already indications that it's becoming cool to be thoughtful, temperate, monogamous. Ironically, the idea that one should govern by speaking softly and carrying a big stick—an African proverb made famous by a white American president—has now been dynamically embodied by an African American head of state.

As Obama prepared to take power, the most famous face in the world seldom reflected the jubilation of all those Americans who took to the streets to exult in their improbable victory. Most often, cameras caught Obama wearing a somber countenance, intently engaged in taking on the problems that faced him. During his victory speech, Obama had spoken movingly of his parents and grandparents, all of whom died before his historic feat. In the days that followed, as I watched televised images of Obama rolling up his sleeves and confronting "the work of remaking this nation," I couldn't help thinking of DuBois, who had thought so deeply and written so astutely about black struggle in America. In *The Souls of Black Folk*, he envisioned the movements of an ambitious black man unfettered by the bonds of racism.

"He would not Africanize America," he wrote, "for America has too much to teach the world and Africa. He would not bleach his Negro soul in a flood of white Americanism, for he knows that Negro blood has a message for the world. He simply wished to make it possible for a man to be both a Negro and an American, without being cursed and spit upon by his fellows, without having the doors of Opportunity closed roughly in his face. This, then, is the end of his striving: to be a co-worker in the kingdom of culture, to escape both death and isolation, to husband and use his best powers and his latent genius."

While this extraordinary, unforgettable time may not be the end of striving, it is, at the very least, a beginning of unparalleled promise.

ACKNOWLEDGMENTS

I BOW DOWN in gratitude to all generations of ancestors in my blood family. As a continuation of my ancestors, I gratefully accept their energy as it flows through me. I ask for their continued support, protection, and strength.

Endless gratitude also:

To my mother, Joyce Smith, for carrying me in her womb for nine months, for calling me Roland Pie and showing me how to write the numeral 4 correctly. To my father, James Irving Smith Jr., for tennis, the homonym game, and pulling me out of that lake. To both of you for never failing to lift me up.

To my siblings: Dale, for T. S. Eliot and James Baldwin; Seitu, for jazz and Tahitian Treat; Karen, for the periodic table and college catalogues; Guy, for baseball and Stacy Adams; Boyce, for the Top 20 and letters from home.

To everyone whose contributions large and small helped animate this humble offering: my mother-in-law, Susie Ward, Mark and Bridgette Arnett, Ralph and Lonnae Parker, Brian and Elanna Gilmore, Jamel and Tracey Richardson, Lester and Shawn Spence, Wil Haygood, Fred and Lisa McKissack, Stephen and Carla Broyles, Natalie Hopkinson, my kind, supportive friends and former colleagues at Book World; Mary Ishimoto Morris, Chris "Topher" Schoppa, Patrick Hadley for timely advice, Ev Small for writing in green ink, Joy Harris, Henry Ferris, Maggie Sivon, Elaine Robnett-Moore, Charles and Paula Nabrit, James and Elsie Richardson, Richard and Ellen MacKenzie, Pier Penic, Rev. Mark Scott, Kevin Powell, Colin Channer, Jeri Peterson, Rohan and Angela Preston, Bashi and Sharayna Rose, Valerie Boyd, Bridget Warren and Todd Stewart, Sylvester and Victoria Brown, Ira Jones, Phil Neely, Thich Nhat Hanh, kingdom principles, Leland Ware, Karima Haynes, David J. Walker, Margena Christian, Kennetta Wainwright, Angelyn Mitchell, Wesley and Marsha Hairston, Mark Trainer and Jennifer Howard, Chris Lehmann and Ana-Marie Cox, Andy Roth, and Valerie Smith (in memoriam).

To the five geniuses: Joseph, G'Ra, Nia, Jelani, and Gyasi.

To my generous fellow scholars at the University of Illinois at Urbana-Champaign, especially Christopher Benson, Sundiata Cha-Jua, Jennifer Hamer, Clarence Lang, and Walt Harrington.

To my patient colleagues at the *Crisis,* including Roger Wilkins, Lottie Joiner, Wayne Fitzpatrick, Sufiya Abdur-Rahman, Michael Freeman, and India Artis.

To anyone whom limited space and memory has caused me to omit, please forgive me and know that I am thankful.